A Short Introduction to the Common Law

A Short Introduction to the Common Law

Geoffrey Samuel

Professor of Law, Kent Law School, UK and Professor affilié, School of Law, Sciences-Po, Paris, France

Edward Elgar
Cheltenham, UK • Northampton, MA, USA

Published by
Edward Elgar Publishing Limited
The Lypiatts
15 Lansdown Road
Cheltenham
Glos GL50 2JA
UK

Edward Elgar Publishing, Inc.
William Pratt House
9 Dewey Court
Northampton
Massachusetts 01060
USA

Paperback edition 2014
Paperback edition reprinted 2015, 2016

A catalogue record for this book
is available from the British Library

Library of Congress Control Number: 2013938970

This book is available electronically in the ElgarOnline.com
Law Subject Collection, E-ISBN 978 1 78254 638 2

ISBN 978 1 78254 637 5 (cased)
ISBN 978 1 78254 950 5 (paperback)

Typeset by Servis Filmsetting Ltd, Stockport, Cheshire
Printed and bound in Great Britain by CPI Group (UK) Ltd, Croydon CR0 4YY

Contents

Figures

Preface

A few years ago Professor Pierre Legrand and I published a short introductory book in France on the common law (Legrand & Samuel, 2008). It was designed primarily for lawyers and other social scientists wishing to gain an insight into the common law institutions and modes of thought. Comparative law students who do not read French have quite frequently asked me whether there is an English translation of the work. There is not. Moreover I found it difficult to recommend any other short book written in English that would serve as a good introduction to the common law for students educated within the civil law tradition. Consequently I decided to write my own short introduction and this book is the result.

It must be stressed that this book is not a translation of our French book. It obviously deals with some of the same subject matter but it is structured very differently and has been written from scratch so to speak. I have also made frequent use of diagrams to explain visually certain aspects of English law. What this book does share with our French book is what might be called the comparative legal studies dimension. That is to say, it is a book that is aimed at students who have been educated in one of the civil law systems and who are now turning their attention to the common law. This said, the book will hopefully be of value to anyone interested in gaining an introductory knowledge to English law.

One word of warning is necessary. Being a shortish book, there is much that is not covered at all – the book does not deal with the criminal law courts and procedure – and some topics are covered only briefly. If there is an emphasis, it is on the historical development of the common-law, non-criminal courts, procedures, remedies and conceptual institutions. Why English law is like it is today is because of its history. Further explanation of the book's substance will be found in the Introduction.

I would like to thank Pierre Legrand for his encouragement with regard to this project and for our many discussions about the civil and common law systems. Thanks are also owed to Ben Booth and colleagues at Edward Elgar for their encouragement, helpful comments and publishing professionalism.

Geoffrey Samuel
Kent Law School
August 2013

Abbreviations

AC	Appeal cases (Third Series)
ADR	Alternative Dispute Resolution
AJCL	American Journal of Comparative Law
All ER	All England Law Reports (Butterworths & Co)
App Cas	Appeal Cases (Second Series)
C	Code of Justinian
CA	Court of Appeal
CC	*Code civil* (French civil code)
Ch	Chancery Division (Third Series)
Ch D	Chancery Division (Second Series)
CJQ	Civil Justice Quarterly
CLJ	Cambridge Law Journal
CLP	Current Legal Problems
CLR	Commonwealth Law Reports
CLS	Critical Legal Studies
CPC	French Code of Civil Procedure
CPR	Civil Procedural Rules
D	Digest of Justinian
DCFR	Draft Common Frame of Reference
EHRLR	European Human Rights Law Review
EHRR	European Human Rights Reports
ER	English Reports
FLR	Family Law Reports
G	Institutes of Gaius
HL	House of Lords
ICLQ	International and Comparative Law Quarterly
IECL	International Encyclopedia of Comparative Law
J	Institutes of Justinian/Justice (High Court)
KB	King's Bench (Third Series)
LC	Lord Chancellor
LJ	Lord Justice (Court of Appeal)
LJCP	Law Journal Common Pleas
LJ Ex	Law Journal Exchequer
LJQB	Law Journal Queen's Bench

Ll Rep	Lloyd's List Law Reports
LQR	Law Quarterly Review
LR CP	Common Pleas Cases (First Series)
LR Eq	Equity Cases (First Series)
LR Ex	Exchequer Cases (First Series)
LR HL	English and Irish Appeals (First Series)
LR QB	Queen's Bench Cases (First Series)
LS	Legal Studies
LT	Law Times Reports
MLR	Modern Law Review
NILQ	Northern Ireland Legal Quarterly
OJLS	Oxford Journal of Legal Studies
OUP	Oxford University Press
P	Probate Division (Third Series)
PC	Privy Council
PL	Public Law
QB	Queen's Bench (Third Series)
QBD	Queen's Bench (Second Series)
RIDC	Revue Internationale de Droit Comparé
RSC	Rules of the Supreme Court
SC	UK Supreme Court
SLR	Statute Law Review
WLR	Weekly Law Reports
ZPO	German Code of Civil Procedure

Table of cases and practice directions

Table of statutory texts

Introduction

There are two major legal traditions in Europe today. The first is the civil law tradition which embraces most of the countries of continental Europe, although some might argue that the Scandinavian systems form their own unit. England, Wales and Ireland do not fall within this civil law family; they are part of the second tradition, namely the common law. What differentiates these two traditions is primarily history. The histories of the civilian legal systems all share the common denominator of Roman law; and the study of the Roman texts has throughout continental Europe from the 11th to the 20th centuries resulted in a particular methodological outlook based on the codification of laws (see generally Stein, 1999). The common law countries do not on the whole share this history or mentality. This is not to say that the common law has remained uninfluenced by the civil law jurists, but because England developed its own particular legal institutions at an early stage (12th–13th centuries) it remained largely immune to the Roman and canon law learning that had blossomed first in Italian universities (11th–14th centuries) and later in French, German and Dutch universities (16th–19th centuries).

One other institutional reason why England remained largely immune to the civilian scholarship was the absence of university law faculties teaching the common law. Indeed before the 19th century there were really only two universities in England, Oxford and Cambridge, and these institutions did not teach the common law until the late 18th century. Thus there was, over many centuries, no corps of university law professors keen to rationalise law as a 'science'. Even in the 19th century when John Austin (1790–1859) started to teach legal science (jurisprudence) at the newly established University College in London he had to abandon the exercise for want of students. 'Lectures on common law topics', write two historians of academic law in the United Kingdom, 'did not, by and large, find a university audience' (Cownie & Cocks, 2009, 6). A Parliamentary Report published in 1846 was particularly damning about the state of legal education in England and Wales and this gradually stimulated, over the following decades, a move towards the establishment of an academic legal community. However it was not until the second half of the 20th century that England and Wales could be said to have a fully functioning corps of university law teachers who were and are involved in scholarship and research.

This underdevelopment applies to the institutions of law as well. A system of royal courts which had been established in the 12th century remained in more or less unreformed operation until the 19th century. Of course there had been important changes in procedures and substantive law; but the fundamentals of the structure remained and even today's courts still bear the imprint of the past. On an ideological level this lack of apparent change helped give the 'common law' its timeless and seamless appeal. Yet, more importantly, it endowed English law with a method-ologically and epistemological (theory of knowledge) dimension which has now become an important characteristic of the common law tradition. The traditional emphasis on cases and case law, before the 19th century, has resulted in a form of reasoning in which facts take a central place and even if legislation is now by far the most important source of law, the circumstances of a case are always of primary importance. Some see this mentality simply as a question of legal style (Zweigert & Kötz, 1998), but others see it as a more fundamental characteristic (Legrand, 1996).

Whatever the situation, a jurist trained in the civil law tradition will find the common law different and legal education in England and Wales (if not in other common law countries as well) will be noticeably distinct when compared to law in a French university (Jamin, 2012, 99–104). This means that one ideal way to teach and to understand English legal insti-tutions and thought is through comparison with aspects of the civilian systems. Difference helps bring out the unique features. Not that much space can be devoted to such a comparative exercise in an introductory work; but where possible the institutions, the procedures, the methods and the theories discussed in relation to English law ought to be compared with those within the continental tradition.

What, then, will be the emphasis in this introductory book? From a comparative viewpoint several characteristics of English law stand out. There is a rather different procedural system – or, at least, there was before the reforms at the end of the 20th century. The differences were once quite fundamental and even today English procedure retains important characteristics inherited from the past. An emphasis on the nature of legal remedies is, perhaps, another important focal point of contrast. Common law remedies must still be differentiated from equitable ones and monetary claims must be differentiated from non-monetary remedies. In terms of legal thought, the common law tradition has undoubtedly imported ideas from the Continent. Indeed one of England's most important theorists, John Austin, went and learned much of his legal theory from the Germans. Nevertheless there are schools of thought in the common law world as a whole – many of which have been of influence in the United Kingdom (Cownie, 2004) – that are considered somewhat radical in France, especially in the way in which they seemingly act as a wedge between university law schools and practice (Jamin, 2012, 105–123). Legal reasoning, at least in appearance, equally seems to be of a different kind than is to be found in a French law school. In truth the differences are complex (Lasser, 2004) and perhaps reflect differing starting points. However, reasoning from precedents, with the emphasis on facts and on analogy, does give rise to more discursive and individualised judgments than reasoning from codes. In England the discovery and application of the law is always a matter of argumentation – of dialectics – whereas reasoning from a strictly authoritative code that traditionally claimed to have no gaps encouraged a much greater structural and inferential approach. Consequently legal thought in England can be said to be distinctive, even if the differences ought not to be exaggerated.

Of course examining in outline the historical and contemporary aspects of procedure, institutions and remedies will not by any means permit one to become an expert on the common law tradition. To become such an expert one must immerse oneself in the cases and their judgments, the statutes and the doctrinal writing. But it will permit, hopefully, both the legal novice and the civilian trained jurist to begin to get a basic insight into the common law mentality and its historical foundation.

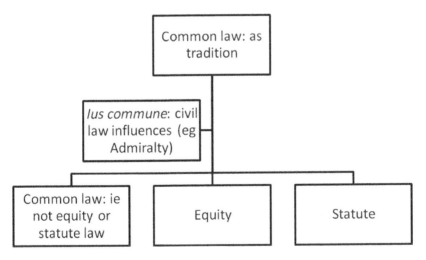

Figure I.1   Different meanings of 'common law'

1. Development of the English courts

The rediscovery of Roman law in the 11th century gave rise to a body of academic doctors in Italy who devoted themselves to commenting upon the Roman texts. These academics, who earned their name Glossators by writing their commentaries as marginal notes ('glosses'), were to lay the foundation for a legal revolution in continental Europe (Berman, 1983). The work on Roman law started by the Glossators was within a few centuries to dominate legal thinking on the Continent and as feudal law became Romanised 'the method, the terminology and even some of the substance of Roman law rubbed off on their *coutumiers*' (van Caenegem). Yet while 'the Glossators mainly busied themselves with the interpretation and systematic exposition of the Roman texts, they knew well enough that much of what they taught had no effective influence outside the doors of the lecture-room' (Jones, 1940, 14). The reason for this is that the living law was the feudal and customary law.

In Britain it was quite a different story in that feudalism provided the context for the development of a customary system that was to resist Roman law not just in substance but also in the methodology and mindset that accompanied the historical process of codification. Unlike the civil law, the tradition of the common law is not associated with a book (the *Corpus Iuris Civilis*). It is, instead, associated with a number of institutions which developed out of the historical facts of their time and which did not necessarily conform to any rational 'plan'. The institutions were functional and they have bequeathed a number of characteristics to the modern common law that are not to be found in the Roman thinking. Accordingly in order to understand the common law one must essentially understand the history of its institutions.

1.1 FEUDAL MODEL

The foundations of the common law undoubtedly reach back to before the Norman invasion of 1066. Nevertheless this event is a good starting point for the history of English law because the Normans created the context in which the main institutions of the common law were to develop and to flourish (Baker, 2002, 12). Certainly the Normans retained not only the legal system that they found in their new country but also the existing administrative and feudal structure. Yet in extending feudalism to the whole of the country and in consolidating the means by which royal power could be asserted the Normans created the context for new developments.

The importance of the feudal structure was that it furnished a political and social context in which the legal concepts of the common law were to form. Indeed it must always be remembered that Roman law was not just a body of rules and legal institutions; it was also an ideological vision of government and society and thus one can talk of a Roman model (Ullmann, 1975, 46–47). The feudal model of government and society was quite different. It did not have at its foundation the two great Roman concepts of *imperium* (state power) and *dominium* (private ownership) and thus did not really adhere to a basic separation between the public and the private. Feudal power was based first on land and then on contract and thus intermixed the ideas of *imperium* and *dominium*. On conquering England, William I claimed the whole country as his and then set about granting large domains to his followers who would in turn bind themselves to him via the feudal contract. They were the tenants-in-chief. Certainly, from the 12th century onwards, nobody actually considered the king to be owner of the country as a matter of social and economic reality; but equally a feudal lord was not an owner of his domain in the Roman sense (Baker, 2002, 230). Each feudal lord would in turn grant parts of his domain to those who swore an oath of allegiance to him and thus governmental power could be said to be based on what was in reality a series of contracts (Ullmann, 1975, 147). Even today land has a special status in English law and so, for example, the word 'goods' does not include real property (see Chapter 6).

In this feudal model the administration of justice was, then, associated with feudal lordship and the Church. However it has to be remembered that the king was also a feudal lord – he was indeed the Lord Tenant in Chief – and as such he was not just integrated directly into the justice system but also entitled to have his own court, which could be used to control inferior tribunals, to assure the King's Peace and to protect his own interests. In addition the king could use his legislative power and his status as the fountain of justice to fashion new remedies, something that Henry II (1133–1189) did to great effect with respect to protecting real rights in land. As mentioned, these real rights were not really forms of ownership but 'seisin', which was closer to a form of possession (see 6.12). However these remedies were to give the emerging common law a very powerful institutional base that would act as one obstacle to the importation of Roman law. The concepts associated with this land law are still at the basis of the modern English law of real property (see Chapter 6).

1.2 FRAGMENTATION OF THE *CURIA REGIS*: THREE COURTS OF COMMON LAW

William I did not arrive just with his army; he also had his King's Household consisting of his advisors and administrators of which he was the head. Gradually this household transformed itself into his Council or Court which became known as the *Curia Regis* and in which various specialist bodies, in particular law and finance, developed. Members of this Council would go on circuit around the country collecting taxes and judging crimes and gradually these specialists became a body of royal judges.

One section, Exchequer (named after its room in which there was a table covered with a cloth resembling a chess board pattern), dealt with finance and taxation and thus consisted of a body of accounting experts. However they found themselves having to judge legal matters arising out of financial issues and at the end of the 12th century a tradition had developed that these experts – the Barons of the Exchequer – would have a lawyer at their head. By the 16th century all the Barons had the status of judges. Yet even in the 12th century the Exchequer had a legal function and two centuries later this function had detached itself from the *Curia Regis*.

Another body of specialists were the advisors to the king. They were involved not just with administration and government but equally with petitions from subjects that affected the king's interests and they would often decide these matters in sessions with the monarch, seated on benches beside him. These became known as hearings in *Coram rege* – the king having a personal jurisdiction to decide cases – and over time the advisors distanced themselves more and more from the monarch, deciding cases in a court that became known as the Bench (*in banco residentes*). From as early as 1268 this court had its own Chief Justice and during the 14th century the Court of King's Bench became detached from the *Curia Regis*, holding sessions in which the king was no longer permitted to sit. Nevertheless, because of its closeness to the king and to government, this court had jurisdiction over matters that were primarily 'public' in their orientation, that is to say administrative law (not that this term existed until relatively recently) and criminal jurisdiction. In fact the boundary between civil and criminal law was not easily perceptible during the 13th and 14th centuries and as a result the judges were able to use the action of trespass – an action that in its origin was more criminal than civil – to extend their jurisdiction into private law. With respect to 'administrative' law, this was not a matter of rules as such; the jurisdiction was rooted in a number of 'prerogative' remedies that were used by King's Bench to control the decisions of inferior tribunals, local authorities and even the other royal courts (see 3.10).

During the reign of Henry II it was normal for the judges to follow the king during his journeys to Bordeaux or to the royal forests. This situation evidently created much inconvenience for litigants and in the early 13th century the lords managed to impose on the then reigning king a 'Great Charter' (*Magna Carta* 1215) in which it was declared that 'common pleas' would be heard by a permanent group of judges in London. At first it was not possible to distinguish between the judges of King's Bench (*Coram rege*) and those hearing Common Pleas (*in banco*); but gradually two separate groups did emerge out of the *Curia Regis* with the result that from the 13th century onwards *Coram rege* became the Court of King's Bench while the judges *in banco* became a third court of common law, the Court of Common Pleas. Until the 16th century Common Pleas was the most important of the common law courts because, as its name suggests, it was dealing with the common litigation between subjects; it became, in other words, the court specialising in 'private' law matters and it increased its jurisdiction by taking cases away from the local courts. However, Common Pleas in turn saw its own jurisdiction reduced by King's Bench and Exchequer, which used legal fictions increasingly to draw ordinary litigation between subjects away from the other court.

Consequently up to the 17th century the common law was a matter of three royal courts competing for litigation. However, during this century the competition between the judges disappeared leaving three royal courts with more or less equivalent jurisdiction, although King's Bench retained its supervisory role while Exchequer continued to specialise in financial matters (Sutton, 1929, 36). These three royal courts lasted until 1875 and the case law that issued from them over the centuries became the 'common law'.

1.3 JURY

While it is perfectly reasonable to refer to these three institutions as courts of justice, they had, in comparison to courts within the civilian tradition, a number of special procedural characteristics of which two need to be mentioned in detail. The first was the jury, which consisted of a group of ordinary subjects drawn from the local community whose role at first was to familiarise the judge on circuit from London with the facts of a crime

(Spencer, 1998, 7–8). They were in effect a group of witnesses in a criminal law trial. Gradually, however, not only did their role change but the distinction between criminal and civil law became more marked and when there was a separation between the two types of trials the same procedure was transferred from criminal to civil procedure. Thus the jury became an institutional element in all common law cases. As for their role, the jury gradually evolved from being a group of witnesses to being a central part of the trial process itself. They became the judges of fact while the judge would (later) decide questions of law. This duality was to remain a central characteristic of the common law trial process until the end of the 19th century and even today the jury has not completely disappeared. It continues to play a central role in serious criminal trials and some civil cases (mainly defamation).

The effects of these late medieval developments were considerable, not only because the members of the jury were for the most part illiterate but also because they were ordinary people with their own livings to pursue. Accordingly cases had to be presented to these non-professionals in a way that they could understand and in a manner that would take days rather than months. Thus the common law 'trial' was oral and efficient time-wise, the idea of a case being based on a written set of documents being impossible. In addition the lawyers had to reduce a case to a series of questions that could be decided by the jury and there developed a set of rigid procedural rules to control this process. Indeed Bracton, a famous 13th-century legal writer, observed that litigation was like a game of chess (Baker, 2002, 77). The result of all this was that the common law largely consisted of knowledge of procedural formulae and so, in the 14th century, there was no body of 'English law' in the same way as there was a body of 'Roman law' (Milsom, 1981, 83). What a lawyer of this period had to know were the appropriate procedures for presenting a case.

1.4 JUDGE AND JURY

Up until the 16th century, then, the central institution was the jury. As for the judge, his role 'could be characterized as having as much in common with that of sports referees as with the proactive role of the modern English judiciary' (Baker, 2003, 49). In other words before the beginning of the 16th century no one looked to litigation as a means of refining the law; indeed 'reasoned final judgments were seldom called for' (Baker, 2003, 50; and see Baker, 2002, 79–80) and there was little separation, in terms of the verdict, between law and fact.

However, this situation was to change during the 16th century. There was growing pressure on the judges to decide points of law, but if this was to happen such decisions had to be removed from the realm of the jury. Such removal became possible thanks to a procedure known as 'in banc' whereby judges in London could, after a jury verdict had been given, consider the matter as a question of law before entering final judgment in the case. At this secondary stage a defendant could apply for a motion on arrest of judgment and this would result in the judges considering the case as a question of law rather than fact and final judgment might be refused on legal grounds. Equally, where there was a verdict for the defendant, judgment would be entered for him unless the plaintiff could show cause as to why such judgment should not be entered. Other motions, such as one for a new trial, subsequently developed with the result that a clear distinction emerged between the role of the jury, as arbiter only of fact, and the role of the judge or judges in banc, as arbiters (and declarers) of law. Accordingly the motion for a new trial put the whole case before the court and resulted in the process whereby a final judicial decision became so important that a majority amongst the judges considering a verdict became the way of achieving it (Baker, 2003, 51). Majority decisions are still the means by which cases are decided on appeal (Kirby, 2007).

This procedure was still much in evidence in the 19th century. Take, for example, the famous contractual damages case of *Hadley v Baxendale* ((1854) 156 ER 145). The plaintiff (claimant) was the owner of a broken mill shaft who arranged for it to be sent speedily to the manufacturers by a firm of transporters (Pickfords). Pickfords delayed the delivery in breach of contract with the result that the mill had to shut down for lack of the shaft. The owners claimed not just ordinary damages (the value of the mill shaft) but compensation for the loss of their profits arising from the closure of the mill. At the trial, the jury awarded damages for the loss of profits but the defendant transporters successfully applied to the Court of Exchequer for a motion for a new trial. The court held that the loss of profit was not recoverable because it was not in the contemplation of the defendant that the mill would have to close if the shaft was delayed. The judgment delivered by the court – and in this case it was a single judgment of the court – remains an important declaration of the law concerning remoteness of damage in contract.

1.5 JUDGES AND JUDGMENT IN CONTEMPORARY ENGLISH LAW

With the disappearance of juries in the 20th century in most non-criminal cases (defamation and fraud are exceptions), the role of fact finding has passed to the trial judge. This has resulted in a rather different situation with respect to the review of these findings of fact because of the duty on judges to give reasons for their decisions, for it 'is a function of due process, and therefore of justice' (*Flannery v Halifax Estate Agencies Ltd* [2000] 1 WLR 377, 381). What is the extent of this duty? Much will depend on the subject matter. As Henry LJ went on to say:

> Where there is a straightforward factual dispute whose resolution depends simply on which witness is telling the truth about events which he claims to recall, it is likely to be enough for the judge (having, no doubt, summarised the evidence) to indicate simply that he believes X rather than Y; indeed there may be nothing else to say. But where the dispute involves something in the nature of an intellectual exchange, with reasons and analysis advanced on either side, the judge must enter into the issues canvassed before him and explain why he prefers one case over the other. This is likely to apply particularly in litigation where as here there is disputed expert evidence; but it is not necessarily limited to such cases (*Flannery*, at 382).

With regard to other questions of fact, and of course to questions of law, the duty to give reasons is based on the idea that without them it would be 'impossible to tell whether the judge has gone wrong on the law or the facts'. Thus 'the losing party would be altogether deprived of his chance of an appeal unless the court entertains an appeal based on the lack of reasons itself' (*Flannery*, at 381).

Yet, as Schiemann LJ pointed out, a judge's task is not an easy one. As he went on to say:

> One does often have to spend time absorbing arguments advanced by the parties which in the event turn out not to be central to the decision-making process. Moreover the experienced judge commonly has thoughts about avenues which it might be crucial to explore but which the parties have not themselves examined. It may be his duty to explore these privately in order to satisfy himself whether they are relevant. Having done the intellectual work there is an understandable temptation to which many of us occasionally succumb to record our thoughts for posterity in the judgment or to refrain from shortening a long first draft (*Customs and Excise Comrs v A* [2003] 2 WLR 210, 82).

Schiemann LJ continued:

> However, judges should bear in mind that the primary function of a first instance judgment is to find facts and identify the crucial legal points and to advance reasons for deciding them in a particular way. The longer a judgment is and the more issues with which it deals the greater the likelihood that: (i) the losing party, the Court of Appeal and any future readers of the judgment will not be able to identify the crucial matters which swayed the judge; (ii) the judgment will contain something with which the unsuccessful party can legitimately

take issue and attempt to launch an appeal; (iii) citation of the judgment in future cases will lengthen the hearing of those future cases because time will be taken sorting out the precise status of the judicial observation in question; (iv) reading the judgment will occupy a considerable amount of the time of legal advisers to other parties in future cases who again will have to sort out the status of the judicial observation in question. All this adds to the cost of obtaining legal advice (para 82).

The disappearance of the jury has, in short, resulted in a significant procedural change of emphasis. Nevertheless it must not be forgotten that the 'role' of the jury has not vanished; it has simply passed to the trial judge.

1.6   WRIT SYSTEM (FORMS OF ACTION)

The second procedural characteristic was the system of writs. This was in its origin simply an administrative process through which a subject gained access to the royal courts and was necessary because these courts were at first exceptional jurisdictions, the administration of justice being the primary concern of the local feudal courts. The *Curia Regis*, within which the common law courts formed, was concerned at first only with the protection of royal and governmental interests, but gradually its jurisdiction was extended as it proved more popular than local justice. Thus the local courts found their jurisdiction being slowly removed in favour of the common law courts (Baker, 2002, 24). Nevertheless litigants never formally had the right to go to the royal courts: they needed a kind of 'ticket' to enter their case and this ticket was the writ which would be obtained from the Chancery section of the *Curia Regis* headed by the Lord Chancellor (Baker, 2002, 53–77).

The writs were a series of formulae that reflected the interests of the king or more generally the typical disputes of the time (the 'common pleas'). The writ of trespass, for example, was originally fashioned to deal with dispossession of land by force of arms (*vi et armis*) while the writ of debt was the means by which an unpaid supplier of goods or a service would obtain his money. Each writ, with its own formula, was based on a model factual situation and once defined became a sort of administrative and legal precedent (Baker, 2002, 55). At the beginning of the 13th century these 'precedents' were to be found in a large book entitled the *Register of Writs* but as the century progressed there was disquiet with its growth not just by the feudal lords, who saw their jurisdiction diminishing, but by the common law judges themselves (there were only 12) who feared being overwhelmed by litigation. As a result the *Register* became closed in that no new writs were permitted, the only exception being the possibility of fashioning writs 'on the case', that is to say analogous to the writ of trespass (Milsom, 1981, 300–305). The consequences of this closure proved fundamental not just to procedure but to English legal thought itself. Access to the common law courts depended on an existing writ within which the litigant could categorise the facts of his case (*non potest quis sine brevi agere* declared a legal maxim of the time); consequently these formulae or 'precedents' came to define the objective law in that they effectively defined a person's 'rights' at law (Baker, 2002, 56). An absence of a suitable writ meant an absence of a legal remedy (*ubi remedium ibi ius*: where there is a remedy there is a right).

This system of writs, or 'forms of action', lasted until the 19th century and before their abolition in 1852 there were more than seventy (for the most important see, for example, Garde, 1841, 1–4, extracted in Samuel, 2007, 510–511). It is of course easy to criticise them as medieval and rigid, but they undoubtedly shaped the common law mentality. They kept legal thinking tied to categories of factual situations and this acted as an obstacle to the methods associated with the civilian jurists of the 16th and 17th centuries (on which see Stein, 1999, 79–82). In other words the system stood in stark contrast to the *mos geometricus* mentality which saw substantive law in terms of a 'logic of norms'; solutions and legal rights were according to this mentality a matter of deduction from a highly coherent model. The common lawyer, instead, used analogy: the facts of a dispute were simply compared to the models of factual situations to be found in the *Register of Writs*.

1.7 DEFECTS OF THE COMMON LAW SYSTEM

Despite the popularity of the royal courts, there were a number of serious defects with respect to the whole system. With one exception (order for the repossession of land), the common law courts could only grant monetary remedies, namely debt and damages. They could not order a party to do something or not to do something (other than to pay a debt or return land to its rightful possessor). The judges themselves were also very conservative and proved largely unwilling in the early centuries of the common law to adapt the law to new circumstances. In addition there were serious defects of procedure, especially with respect to the rigidity of the forms of action; if, for example, a claimant chose the wrong writ he risked seeing his whole case fail on the ground of want of form (for a 19th century example see *Jacobs v Seward* (1872) LR 5 HL 464). The procedure was equally rigid with respect to documents under seal: the common law judges refused to look beyond the seal to see if there was fraud or duress. And of course the jury was hardly the best of institutions when it came to litigation based on documentary evidence. In fact once a jury had given its verdict it was very difficult to appeal against this decision, for there was no proper system of appeal courts over and above the three courts of common law. Added to all this, were the problems of delay and corruption.

1.8   COURT OF CHANCERY AND THE SYSTEM OF EQUITY

One possibility open to a disgruntled litigant in the 13th and 14th centuries was to petition the king directly since he remained the source (the 'fountain') of all justice. From the 14th century onwards the king would pass these petitions to his Lord Chancellor whose role was to be the 'keeper of the king's conscience', as well as being, of course, the head of the judicial section of the *Curia Regis*. In turn this high-ranking officer would often take advice from the royal judges before responding to a petition. This whole procedure attracted the name 'Equity'. However at the end of the 15th century the Lord Chancellor had started to decide these petitions in his own name using as a guide a mixture of his Christian discretion (since before the 16th century most Lord Chancellors were ecclesiastics), canon law and Roman law. Gradually the Lord Chancellor moved from being an individual taking decisions to a royal court dispensing justice in the name of the king. To the three common law courts was added a fourth court, the Court of Chancery, and the case law issuing from this court became known as equity.

At first the duality functioned, on the whole, in a co-operative fashion but in the 17th century a conflict developed, above all between the Lord Chief Justice Coke and the Lord Chancellor Lord Ellesmere (Lord Chancellor from 1596 to 1617). This was a serious crisis which was only settled when Lord Ellesmere convinced the king, James I, to intervene in favour of equity: when rules of common law and equity came into conflict those of equity would prevail (see now Senior Courts Act 1981, s 49). After the death of Ellesmere, his successors re-established cordial relations with the common law judges. Moreover, from the 17th century onwards, the Lord Chancellors progressively came to regard equity less as a multitude of decisions founded upon conscience and more a body of principles (van Caenegem, 1999). Yet these principles were never seen as being in opposition to those of the common law; the whole point of the Court of Chancery and its system of principles and remedies was to fill the gaps existing as a result of the defaults of the common law. In particular, of course, there was in the common law courts the lack of non-monetary remedies together with the rigidity of the forms of action and the jury system.

The Court of Chancery accordingly used a quite different procedural model, one perhaps closer to the *ius commune* pattern to be found on the Continent (see Baker, 2003, 180–181 and 2.1). There were, then, no writs and no juries and it tackled the shortcomings of the common law through the development of a range of new remedies of which the most important was the injunction. This was a negative order made by the court against a party in person (*in personam*) not to do something and it could be employed to stop a litigant pursuing his rights at common law if such an act appeared to the Lord Chancellor as being an abuse of power or rights. In addition to the injunction, equity developed other non-monetary remedies such as specific performance of contracts, rescission of transactions and rectification of documents. In other words, the Court of Chancery developed remedies that could look behind documents and the like to see if there had been fraud, mistake, duress or undue influence (for a modern example see *Daventry DC v Daventry & District Housing Ltd* [2012] 1 WLR 1333).

In addition to these new remedies the Court of Chancery was able to fashion some new institutions (often indirectly through the use of injunctions) such as the trust. In the late Middle Ages an owner of land would frequently transfer it to another to be held 'on trust' for the benefit of a third person. The common law courts would look only at the form of the transfer and thus not recognise the 'trust' obligation attaching to the new owner. The Lord Chancellor took a quite different position on the basis of the King's Conscience and would force the new proprietor (the trustee) to respect his obligations towards the third party (the beneficiary). Gradually this position changed from being a matter of equitable remedies to one of property rights; the beneficiary acquired under a trust a real right in the trust property and there thus developed two forms of 'ownership', one at common law and one in equity.

1.9 COMMERCIAL LAW

The shortcomings of the common law might seem surprising in the context of the importance, today, of commerce to English law. The procedural rigidity and remedial limitations would hardly seem attractive to the merchants of the late Middle Ages. In fact, before the 18th century an important part of mercantile law was not to be found in the royal courts but in the Court of Admiralty and, before that, in the merchants' own courts.

The Court of Admiralty was partly the result of a jurisdictional limitation that attached to a jury, which could not be convened with respect to a case that happened outside of England. This gap was at first filled by the *Curia Regis* and then by several specialised courts of which Admiralty was the most important. This was a court that formed around the Lord High Admiral who was the head of the navy and who had jurisdiction over piracy. Later this jurisdiction was extended to the law of the sea and then to commercial law in general, guided by judges trained in Roman and civil law. There were two reasons why Admiralty was able to capture this work from the old mercantile courts. First, it employed the fiction that any commercial case happened *super altum mare* and thus it simply pretended that the law of the sea and commercial law were one and the same. Secondly, to some extent, these two areas were one and the same since England was a sea-faring nation. Even today many commercial cases involve shipping and this was particularly true in the 18th and 19th centuries. However the success was not to last and from the 17th century Admiralty found itself gradually being relieved of its jurisdiction by the common law courts.

The common law courts were able to attract this commercial work because of several important developments. First, the law itself had matured at the level of theory; in particular a remedy based on the notion of trespass had been extended to cover damage caused by a person failing to do what he had promised. This new action of *assumpsit* in effect provided a compensation claim for a party who had been the victim of a breach of contract even although in the 17th century there was no theory of contract in the civilian sense of the term (see 7.2). Secondly, the Lord Chief Justice Coke had attacked the Court of Admiralty with Writs of Prohibition which had the effect of suppressing litigation in this court and attracting some of it to the common law courts. Thirdly, in the 18th century, Lord Mansfield, a common law judge, succeeded in adapting the procedures of the common law to the needs of the commercial classes with the result that commercial law got absorbed into the common law (or vice versa as some think).

All through the 19th century the common law courts built upon these developments and succeeded not just in fashioning a general law of contract but in developing specific areas of commercial law such as charterparty and insurance contracts. This is the reason why the common law is regarded by many as a commercial law (Moréteau, 2000, para 8). In 1875 the Court of Admiralty was absorbed into the Probate, Divorce and Admiralty Division of the High Court and in 1970, when this Division became the Family Division, Admiralty was absorbed into the Queen's Bench Division (Administration of Justice Act 1970, s 1). Thus Admiralty was finally merged with the common law at both the substantive and the formal levels. However an Admiralty Court remains as a separate court within the Queen's Bench Division.

Nevertheless these 19th- and 20th-century developments did not result in a system that was perfectly suited to the needs of the commercial community. At the end of the 19th century a commercial court was constituted within the Queen's Bench Division of the High Court with the aim of speedily and efficiently dealing with commercial cases. But even this development seems not to have overcome problems of delay and expense with the result that, during the 20th century, arbitration was drawing commercial matters away from the courts (*Report of the Committee on Supreme Court Practice and Procedure*, Cmnd 8878, 1953, para 895). Today arbitration is not seen in a negative light and indeed has been given legislative support (Arbitration Act 1996). Moreover, the commercial court has embraced Alternative Dispute Resolution (ADR) procedures whereby parties are encouraged to resolve their dispute through mediation (see *Halsey v Milton Keynes General NHS Trust* [2004] 1 WLR 3002 and 1.13).

1.10   REFORM OF THE COMMON LAW IN THE 19TH CENTURY

Despite these important adaptations within the common law system, the beginning of the 19th century nevertheless saw England with a set of courts and procedures that were feudal and medieval in origin. In the age of science all this was to seem somewhat irrational and from a litigant's point of view it probably was. Why were there three courts of common law with equivalent jurisdiction? Why were there two systems of legal rules, law and equity? Why was there no proper appeal structure? Why was there so much emphasis on the form rather than the substance of a legal claim? In addition there were the scandals associated with delay in the Court of Chancery (see Dickens's *Bleak House*).

The 19th century was accordingly to become the age of reform. In 1830 a Court of Exchequer Chamber was established to act as a court of error, that is to say as a kind of appeal court; the new court consisted of judges from the common law courts other than the one from which the appeal came. This idea of error was the result of the old writ of error which had been one means of appeal within the common law system, along with the procedure for a motion for a new trial. A jury verdict could be overturned if an error was discovered in the legal record of the case. In fact the 1830 court was not the first Exchequer Chamber to have appeared: there had been three others over the centuries, though none had found long-term success (see figure 1.1). In 1851 the legislature established a Court of Appeal in Chancery which was set up as a true appeal court – that is to say to rehear a case – rather than as a court of error (see figure 1.2). In addition to these institutional reforms, Parliament set about reforming the law of procedure. The forms of action were effectively abolished by the Common Law Procedure Act 1852 and some progress was made in fusing law and equity with respect to remedies and the ability of a single court to have recourse to both systems. In 1846 a system of local county courts was established. At first the jurisdiction of these new courts was restricted, but their increasing popularity encouraged the progressive extension of this jurisdiction with the result that today the county courts play a major role in the English civil law system. Another procedural change that was to have an important long-term effect was the power granted to a judge to dispense with a jury in civil claims; by the middle of the 20th century it had virtually disappeared from non-criminal cases, its role having been taken over by the trial judge (*Ward v James* [1966] 1 QB 273).

To a certain extent, then, the procedural and institutional mentality of the Court of Chancery was, thanks to these legislative reforms, imposing itself on the common law (Baker, 2002, 141–142). As for the Court of Chancery itself, there had been a number of important reforms since the beginning of the 19th century. The Lord Chancellor gradually decided fewer and fewer cases at first instance and in 1851 a Court of Appeal in Chancery was established. A few years later statute gave judges the power to award damages in lieu of an injunction or specific performance (Chancery Amendment Act 1858; see *Jaggard v Sawyer* [1995] 2 All ER 189). From then on it was possible to obtain damages (in equity) without having to go to another court if refused an equitable remedy.

1.11   JUDICATURE ACT 1875

However, the principal reform of the English legal system came in 1875 with the Judicature Acts 1873–75 (Supreme Court of Judicature Acts 1873 and 1875). These statutes swept away the old system of central courts and established a new model called the Supreme Court which operated at two levels. The first level was the High Court, which consisted of an amalgamation of the three old common law courts, the Court of Chancery, the Court of Admiralty and the ecclesiastical courts. The High Court was the court of first instance and had (after 1881) three divisions: the Queen's Bench Division (QBD), Chancery Division (ChD) and the Probate, Divorce and Admiralty Division (PDA), this last consisting of all those old courts that had largely dispensed Roman and civil law.

In 1970 this third Division was abolished and replaced by the Family Division (Administration of Justice Act 1970, s 1). Most cases were to be heard by a single judge who would decide (if there was no jury) both questions of fact and of law; however there were also Divisional Courts, often with two judges, of which the most important were those of the QBD, deciding questions of law arising from the magistrates' courts and deciding questions of administrative law.

The second level of the Supreme Court consisted of the Court of Appeal. This new appeal court took as its model not the old Court of Exchequer Chamber but the Court of Appeal in Chancery; it was therefore a genuine appeal court and not a court of error (Baker, 2002, 141–142). Normally a case would come before three judges and each had the right to issue his (or her) own judgment, although sometimes there would be a joint one issued as the judgment of the court (now quite frequent). This Court of Appeal was originally envisaged as being the first and final appeal; thus further appeal to the House of Lords (which had jurisdiction to hear appeals thanks to its old *Curia Regis* status) was to be abolished. However, between 1873 and 1875 there was a change of government with the result that a decision was made to retain the House of Lords as an appeal court. Consequently the old three-level structure (common law or Chancery court, appeal or error court and then the House of Lords) was ultimately retained, although statute ensured that the judicial section of the House of Lords was turned into a proper appeal body staffed by fully qualified Lords of Appeal (Appellate Jurisdiction Act 1876).

A much more recent development with respect to the House of Lords as an appeal body is in respect of its name. It has become the Supreme Court (thus necessitating a change with respect to the 1875 Supreme Court) and is housed in a building independent of the House of Lords itself (Constitutional Reform Act 2005). Mention must also be made of the Privy Council as an appeal court. This became independent of the *Curia Regis* in the 16th century with jurisdiction to decide appeals coming from overseas colonies and this was formalised by legislation during the 19th century (Judicial Committee Acts 1833 and 1844). It also heard appeals from the ecclesiastical courts and from the Court of Admiralty and is staffed by Lords of Appeal (now justices of the new Supreme Court).

1.12 DEVELOPMENT OF TRIBUNALS

In addition to the system of ordinary civil process courts (High Court and county court), the 20th century saw the development of a system of tribunals. These tribunals were created by statute and largely dealt with disputes arising between citizen and various public authorities. Thus they resembled to some extent the administrative courts to be found in the civil law tradition. The development of these dispute resolution institutions outside the normal court system was not uncontroversial, but they had a number of advantages such as speed, expertise and less formality. They were also very diverse, not just in respect of their subject matter – taxation, social security, rent, licensing and so on – but also in their procedures. There were around 70 different tribunals. Some of these were like courts with court-like procedures, others were less formal; there were also differences with respect to the possibility of appeals (see *Report of the Committee on Tribunals and Inquiries*, Cmnd 218, 1957, paras 35–37). One major criticism that attached to this system of tribunals was that they were resourced and staffed by the public authority or department which administered the scheme and thus the tribunal appeared not to be sufficiently independent and neutral. Accordingly the system was reformed to some extent in 1958 and the great majority of tribunals were made subject both to an appeal route to the High Court and to control by judicial review proceedings (see 3.12) (Tribunals and Inquiries Act 1958).

The present century has seen further and major reform. The Tribunals, Courts and Enforcement Act 2007 has created a new unified structure of tribunals which, in its structural pattern, resembles in outline (or by analogy) the two-tier system of the old Supreme Court established by the Judicature Act 1873. There is a First-tier Tribunal which is divided into various chambers and an Upper Tribunal, also organised into chambers; both of these tiers are staffed by judges as well as by lay members, the Upper Tribunal actually consisting of High Court judges. However, as Lady Hale has pointed out, although the 'new structure may look neat . . . the diversity of jurisdictions accommodated means that it is not as neat as it looks' (*R (Cart) v Upper Tribunal* [2012] 1 AC 663, 23). For example, the Upper Tribunal is certainly an appeal court in the full sense of the term, but it is equally a court of first instance for some matters and it is not too clear why some of these matters should be assigned to this superior tier while others are not (Lady Hale, para 23).

It would appear, therefore, that there now are two parallel court systems in the UK rather than one court system and a mode of ADR via tribunals. As a result of the 2007 Act there exists something of a separate corps of judges under the responsibility of a Senior President (see Lady Hale, para 22) with the consequence that the idea of a unique common law court system covering both private and public law matters might have to be rethought. It could be that there really is now a 'system of specialised administrative courts' (Boyron, 2010, 126).

1.13 ALTERNATIVE DISPUTE RESOLUTION

It has already been noted that the tribunals are a form of ADR in that they represent an alternative to the ordinary courts. However, tribunals are not the only form of ADR; other forms are arbitration, mediation, negotiation and the ombudsman (or now ombud, ombudsperson). These alternative forms have become increasingly important since the Woolf Report (see 2.3), which felt that many disputes could be resolved through mediation (and see *Cowl v Plymouth CC* [2002] 1 WLR 803, 1–3), but there were important advances taking place before the reforms. Mediation has been developed in the Commercial Court (Commercial Court Practice Direction [1994] 1 All ER 34) and is seen as of particular value in family law disputes (Family Law Act 1996, s 8). There is even a mediation scheme attached to the Court of Appeal. One problem is whether this form of ADR should be compulsory; the Court of Appeal has indicated reluctance to penalise parties who refuse mediation since this could amount to interfering with the right of access to a court (*Halsey v Milton Keynes General NHS Trust* [2004] 1 WLR 3002) but the decision has attracted criticism. Whatever the position on costs, it is likely that mediation will become an increasingly important form of ADR.

Mediation does have both a long history and a vital comparative dimension. In terms of history it is associated with particular communities such as those founded on religious beliefs, but more recently it has gained in importance in areas such as the professional, employment, landlord and tenant, and consumer environments. No doubt these community- and interest-based groups can provide a rich source for research. Equally some countries like China can offer much potential to legal anthropologists and comparatists given the country's long cultural tradition of mediation as a dispute resolution process (see Roberts & Palmer, 2005). There are however problems with processes such as mediation. Is it actually effective in terms of its take-up rate? The research so far is by no means conclusive. Indeed, there is even a powerful argument to be made against forced, or partially forced, settlements which might result from ADR (Fiss, 1984). There are other difficulties as well. Such methods often function in the 'shadow of the law' with the result that there is a permanent threat of 'juridification', especially as mediation is operating within an atomised ideology of rights (see 5.4–6 on Dworkin). Yet this juridification is itself weakened by the lack of any precedent system. Furthermore, the process can be manipulated by state power for reasons of economic efficiency and this may mean that it ends up operating as an adjunct to the ordinary court procedures (justice on the cheap). The historical and comparative possibilities can even have a negative effect in as much as there is a temptation to introduce mediation procedures by way of transplantation from one society to another without proper consideration of cultural context. These are by no means fatal problems, but they do indicate that teaching and research, which perhaps is lacking at the moment in law schools because of the emphasis on positive law, needs to take ADR much more seriously.

Arbitration of course has a long history dating back to Roman law and in England it has now been put on a secure statutory basis (Arbitration Act 1996). This Act is said to represent a new philosophy in that recourse from arbitration decisions to the courts has become difficult, thus making arbitration more independent of the court system (*Lesotho Highlands Development Authority v Impregilo SpA* [2006] 1 AC 221). The advantages can be summarised under the 'four S's', namely saving, secrecy, speciali-sation and speed; but these aims and objectives are not always achieved. Some disputes can end up, for example, costing as much as litigation. The actual basis for arbitration is contract and many commercial and consumer contracts will contain arbitration clauses; the actual validity of these clauses is not, however, dependent upon the validity of the contract itself (Arbitration Act 1996, s 7). In many respects arbitration is like litiga-tion and so arbitrators are under a duty to act fairly and impartially and to give reasons for their decisions; the remedies available are similar to those available in the ordinary courts. Nevertheless, despite these processes in some ways mirroring the ordinary court system, the great advantage of arbitration is that arbitrators can be specialists in the area in which the dispute has arisen. Ordinary judges are not likely to be experts in, say, the chocolate trade.

As for the ombudsmen schemes, these are now well established in both the public and the private sector since the creation of the Parliamentary Commissioner in 1967 to investigate claims of governmental maladminis-tration (Parliamentary Commissioner Act 1967). Other ombudsmen have been established to investigate, for example, the health service and local government. In the private sector there are now ombudsmen covering a range of commercial and consumer activities, for example banking and insurance, pensions, telecommunications and estate agents. There are said to be three essential features that define an ombudsman: he or she is an independent and non-partisan officer who deals with specific com-plaints from the public and who has the power to investigate, criticise and publicise injustice and maladministration (Verkuil, 1975). One important feature that emerges from this definition is that the ombudsman, at least in the public sector, has no power to reverse an unjust decision and her decisions are not binding; the primary weapons are persuasion and publi-cation. This can lead to serious difficulty when the government refuses to act on a report. Complaints to the Parliamentary Commissioner cannot be made directly; they have to go first to the complainant's Member of Parliament (MP) who may or may not refer the matter to the ombudsman. In other words there is a filter device, which in turn means that the MP becomes part of the dispute resolution process. However, this filter device does not apply to the National Health Service or the Local Government Ombudsman, nor does it apply in the private sector schemes. The Law Commission has recommended a number of important reforms, including the abolition of the filter process and of the non-binding nature of the ombudsman's findings (Law Com: Public Service Ombudsmen, Law Com 329, 2011). In the private sector the powers of the ombudsman are stronger and so, for example, the financial services ombudsman can order a company to pay money and (or) put things right (Financial Services and Markets Act 2000, s 229). These schemes are a valuable alternative to litigation.

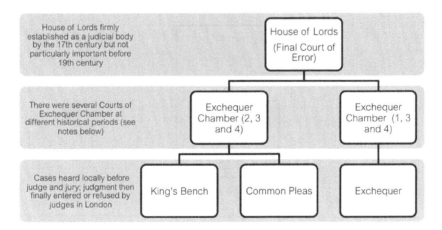

Notes:
1. Exchequer Chamber (1): This court of error was created in 1357 to hear error cases from the Court of Exchequer.
2. Exchequer Chamber (2): This court of error was created in 1585 to hear error cases from King's Bench. Error cases from Common Pleas were heard in King's Bench.
3. Exchequer Chamber (3): This was not really a court as such but an informal gathering of judges from the 15th to the 17th century who would discuss difficult cases.
4. Exchequer Chamber (4): In 1830 Parliament created a court of error to hear cases from all three common law courts. A further appeal could be taken to the House of Lords (see eg *Rylands v Fletcher* (1866) LR 1 Ex 265 (Ex); (1868) LR 3 HL 330 (HL).
5. By the 17th century the House of Lords had become established as a final court of error from the Courts of Exchequer Chamber.

Figure 1.1   Courts of Exchequer Chamber

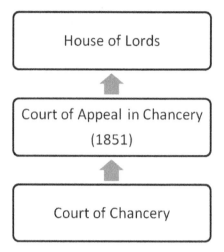

Figure 1.2   Equity court structure

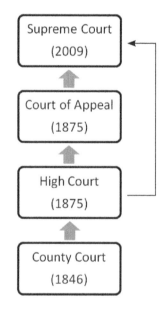

Notes:
1. There is no automatic right to appeal to the Court of Appeal or the Supreme Court. Permission to appeal is required.
2. It is possible to appeal directly from the High Court or to the Supreme Court (leapfrogging procedure); but this is rarely used.

Figure 1.3   Contemporary court structure (non-criminal)

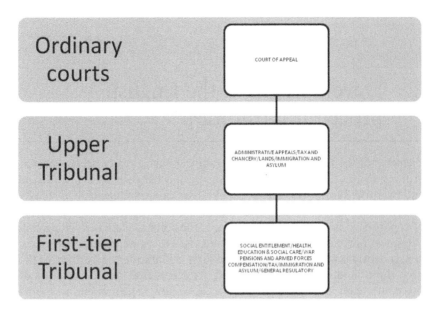

Figure 1.4   Tribunals

2. Development of the English procedural tradition

Elements of the English procedural tradition have already been indicated in the previous chapter, for a clear separation between legal institutions and the procedural forms that attach to them cannot realistically be made. Nevertheless much more needs to be said about the history and philosophy of civil procedure if an understanding of the common law is to be gained. Moreover procedure is an area that lends itself to a comparative approach; consequently it will perhaps be useful, first, to indicate the outlines of the procedural model that has dominated in the civil law. An appreciation of this continental model will permit one to see how the common law model is different and how these differences are in fact part of the characteristic elements of English civil procedure. However this is not to suggest that the two models do not share common ideas.

2.1 COMPARATIVE EXCURSUS: THE DEVELOPMENT OF CONTINENTAL LEGAL PROCEDURE

'The Romano-canonical procedure is one of the wonders of legal history', claims Professor van Caenegem; 'it was not based on a haphazard accumulation of unrelated remedies, dominated by different rules according to the moment of their creation' (1971, para 19). The main features, as described by van Caenegem (1971, para 15), of this Romano-Canonical procedure were as follows. There was a single professional judge who investigated the complaint in an active inquisitorial manner. Proceedings were in writing (*quod non est in actis non est in mundo*: if it is not in the file it does not exist) and they were opened with a written libel (*libellus*) delivered by plaintiff to judge. The defendant could invoke various *exceptiones* while the witnesses were examined by *interrogatores*. The whole procedure was marked by formal stages (especially the *litis contestatio*) which amounted to a cohesive system in itself; judgments, of course, were always on the written case.

Appeals were possible within the Church and, later, state hierarchy, and such appeals, in theory and often in practice, could end up in the hands of the Pope or the king. This procedure was 'undemocratic' in the sense that it was entirely bureaucratic and involved only professionals; yet it quickly came to dominate in France, Italy and Spain. In Germany it followed the reception of Roman law and only in England did it fail to dominate, although procedure in the Court of Chancery, so very different from that of the common law, did resemble it. After the Middle Ages the main characteristics of the Romano-canonical model were preserved by legislation or by the courts themselves (for example in the *Parlement de Paris*) and thus the model's main features became imprinted on the great codes of procedure in the 19th century (see van Caenegem, 1971, paras 91–92, 132–134). In addition to the Romano-canonical procedure itself, the history of particular aspects of procedure (for example, types of Roman actions, the notion of judgment, role of the judge, proof) and the effect that these have had on substantive rights is of importance in understanding the civilian mentality.

How, then, can this historical procedural model be summed up? Legal procedure in the civil law tradition can be described as follows: 'A single judge, a professional with academic training, received the complaints, heard the parties and the witnesses, saw the documents, decided on questions of fact and of law and gave judgement according to his conviction (in a later stage this was altered by the theory of legal proof . . .)'. In addition these 'judgments were liable to appeal along the hierarchical ladder' (van Caenegem, 1971, para 15). This procedural model attracted the name 'Romano-canonical' because, as the term implies, it was based on the structure to be found in the *Corpus Iuris Civilis* (the Roman law texts rediscovered in the 11th century) as modified by the work of the canon lawyers of the late Middle Ages. The edifice was built around the inquisitorial model whereby a judge took control *ex officio* of a case and opened an inquiry on receiving a written *libellus*. This inquiry then became part of a segmental and unfolding process in which judgment was reached only after a long series of separate stages which might literally have lasted a lifetime. Part of the delay problem was caused by the sharp procedural divide between judge and parties. Although the judge might have had a more active role in the investigation, this role became diminished as the emphasis on writing increased. The judge lost control of the proceedings in private law and the conduct of the proceedings itself was exclusively in the hands of the parties (Cappelletti & Garth, 1986, para 3). There was an important ideological logic to this development as well: private litigation was considered a private affair and this was the dominant paradigm in continental procedure up until the 19th century.

With the coming of the modern era there was, needless to say, a break with the *ius commune* past. In the French model, to take a central example, the reliance on writing and inquisitorial methods gave way to a greater role for 'orality' (*plaidoiries, débat oral*) and many fewer segments with the result that legal cases unfolded more rapidly and were less constrained by formal rules and regulations concerning the taking of evidence, the hearing of arguments and the formulation of decisions (Cappelletti & Garth, 1986, para 4). Equally there was a return to the more active role of the judge. Accordingly, although it is a fundamental principle of continental civil procedure that a judge can never commence legal proceedings on his own motion (*nemo judex sine actore*), once the parties have started an action the judge has power to, and may be required to, make enquiries on his own motion. Indeed 'party control over civil proceedings is being reduced by the fact that wider and wider powers of investigation are being given to the examining judge, and even to the trial judges' (Kohl, 1982, para 129). Accordingly one can say that an emphasis on the written file (*dossier*), on an unfolding process (*le déroulement du procès*) and on an active role for the judge (*instruction*) remain important characteristics not just of French, but of continental civil procedure (Cappelletti & Garth, 1986, paras 3, 5).

2.2 THE DEVELOPMENT OF ENGLISH CIVIL PROCEDURE

If one returns to the English common law and to its history, this tradition developed its own specific form of procedure quite separate from the Romano-canonical model to be found in the countries of the reception of Roman law. This English procedure had distinct characteristics. In particular it was an oral procedure because decisions of fact were not made by judges learned in Roman law and trained in the university faculties; they were made by juries which consisted of ordinary people who were often illiterate. To the Roman and canon lawyers of the late Middle Ages the idea that 'the decisive verdict in a law case' might be put 'in the power of a dozen illiterate rustics' was considered 'as utterly ridiculous and absurd' (van Caenegem, 1987, 119; see *R v Young* [1995] QB 324). Yet the jury was to dominate the civil procedure of English private and criminal law up until the end of the 19th century and even today, in order to understand the structure of the legal process, it is necessary to imagine *le jury fantôme* in every tort and contract case (Jolowicz). The rigid distinction between the trial and pretrial process and between questions of fact and questions of law results from the existence of the jury. Moreover, once the jury had issued its verdict, appeal against the decision was in theory almost impossible and in practice difficult. Jury trials are now rare in private law cases in England (*Ward v James* [1966] 1 QB 273). However in the United States they still have a central role and thus present special problems when it comes to appeals (Herzog & Karlen, 1977, paras 44–48).

In the common law system, because of the illiteracy of the jury, the trial was, and to an important extent remains today, an oral process (although there have been recent and fundamental reforms). Witnesses are heard in court and their evidence is open to examination and cross-examination by the parties' lawyers (*Final Report of the Committee on Supreme Court Practice and Procedure*, Cmnd 8878, 1953, para 365). In such a process it is not for the judge to question the witnesses since his or her role is largely passive; indeed too many interruptions by a judge once gave rise to grounds for appeal (*Jones v National Coal Board* [1957] 2 QB 55). However, this is subject to qualification. First, this passive role applies only to the hearing of evidence; when it comes to arguments of law the judge will assume a much more active (or reactive) approach with regard to the parties' arguments. Secondly, recent reforms have resulted in the judges having a more active general role (Andrews, 2000) and documents are becoming ever more central. One might add a third qualification. In family law cases – especially those involving children – the idea of a completely passive judge silently listening to the evidence from both sides is an unrealistic image. Nevertheless an important characteristic of the common law is the practical skill of dealing with evidence both at the pretrial and the trial stage and this is something that is primarily in the hands of the parties' lawyers and their cross-examination of witnesses. Fact handling, to put it another way, helps give the common law its empirical flavour and helps shift the emphasis off the idea that legal knowledge is a matter of highly systematised rules.

Nevertheless an emphasis on facts does not necessarily mean an absence of formality: proceedings were once dominated by the form of the action and this mentality is still to be found on occasions with respect to pleadings (*Esso v Southport Corporation* [1956] AC 218, 238, 241). French judges would appear to have greater freedom, although since the Woolf reforms of 1998 (see below) the position in England has probably changed to a considerable extent (see *McPhilemy v Times Newspapers Ltd* [1999] 3 All ER 775, 792–793). Another characteristic of the common law model is the emphasis on the private interests of the parties rather than on the public interest of the legal process (*Air Canada v Sec of State* [1983] 2 AC 394, 438). However, once again, the recent procedural reforms give the judges much more control and the emphasis is now on 'the abstract interests of justice' (see Andrews, 2000, 34).

More generally the procedural position in the common law can be summed up as follows: 'There is immediacy in the relationship between the parties, counsel and witnesses, and the adjudicating judge or jury, and there is generally concentration of proceedings into one hearing or a series of hearings held in the shortest possible period of time' (Cappelletti & Garth, 1986, para. 7). This contrasts sharply with the Romano-canonical model. However, the reaction against the reliance upon an entirely written procedure over the last century and the adoption of oral proceedings would seemingly bring continental civil procedure closer to that of England. This apparent *rapprochement* becomes even more credible when it is appreciated that procedure in Chancery, which became the model for the common law courts in 1875, was always closer to the civilian model than to the common law one. One might add that recent reforms in English civil procedure take the common law even closer to the French model (Jolowicz, 1996); the pretrial proceedings will be under the strict control of a judge (Andrews, *op cit*).

Yet the differences of history have shaped mentality. In England the emphasis on argumentation (before a jury) has endowed the law with a particular flavour. It is knowledge to be discovered, not by the court as such, as is (at least in theory) the case in the civil law (*da mihi factum, dabo tibi ius*; *jura novit cura*: the court knows the law), but by a debate between plaintiff counsel, defendant counsel and the judge (the judge, as we have mentioned, is not passive when it comes to arguments of law). Moreover there is a tradition, resulting from the role of the jury, that witnesses should be seen and heard by the trial judge (see *Final Report of the Committee on Supreme Court Practice and Procedure*, Cmnd 8878, 1953, para 365). Judgments, accordingly, often reflect this style. In the civil law the scientific nature of the whole process has given rise to a different style of judgment which traditionally repressed the open-ended and argumentative nature of legal knowledge (see *Final Report*, 1953, *supra*, paras 250–252).

2.3   REFORM OF ENGLISH CIVIL PROCEDURE

The Judicature Act of 1875 represented the break between the old common law system of courts and the new model. The structure put in place by this legislation is more or less the one that is to be found in England and Wales today even if there have been some further major reforms. However what is particularly interesting about these modern reforms is that some of them are aimed at what might be described as the traditional procedural philosophy of the common law trial process.

As we have seen, there have been a number of reforms to the English legal system throughout the 20th century, but major change belongs more to the period that might broadly be described as the turn of the last century, that is to say the period from 1990 onwards. The reforms of this latest period have largely resulted from concerns about a number of procedural and institutional aspects of the English justice system.

Towards the end of the 20th century the government appointed a senior judge, Lord Woolf, to head an enquiry and in 1996 he produced a report entitled *Access to Justice* in which he proposed some radical reforms (Woolf, 1996). The judge emphasised a number of defects to be found in civil procedure – excessive delay, high costs, complexity and outdated terminology – but he equally criticised the whole philosophy of the trial system in the English common law. Perhaps this philosophy had been summed up by a comment from a Law Lord a quarter of a century ago: 'In a contest purely between one litigant and another', said Lord Wilberforce, 'the task of the court is to do, and be seen to be doing, justice between the parties', for there 'is no higher or additional duty to ascertain some independent truth' (*Air Canada v Secretary of State for Trade* [1983] 2 AC 394, 438). What this comment reflects is the traditional nature of the common law trial system in which the judge presides, even with the disappearance of the jury, over an oral process lasting perhaps just a few days (maybe even shorter but sometimes in fact longer). Even in this role the judge's duty was – and indeed remains – passive. It is the parties' barristers who call and question the witnesses. The judge, then, is an arbiter and not a controller; he or she decides the questions of fact only with respect to those facts presented to him or her in the courtroom. It is the same with regard to the law. The English judge does not normally do his or her own legal research but decides questions about the law and its application to the facts from legal argument presented to him or her by the barristers (or now solicitors). It is the barristers who are charged with researching the relevant law and they are under a strict professional duty to the court to do this accurately and in good faith (*Copeland v Smith* [2000] 1 WLR 1371).

What worried Lord Woolf about this philosophy was that it seemed to encourage the parties to litigation not 'to put their cards on the table' so to speak. As a result he proposed in his report that the phase before the trial – the pretrial proceedings – should be governed by a judge who was a specialist in case management. Traditionally this phase was a matter only for the parties – or more usually their solicitors – and this meant that there was often an interest in creating delays and accumulating costs. Lord Woolf also proposed that there should be a single set of procedural rules covering both the High Court and the county courts and that there should be several procedural 'tracks' depending on the complexity of the litigation and the amount of the claim. For the simplest cases Lord Woolf proposed the use of the small claims procedure before a district judge in the county court, such an action attracting an informal procedure. If the sum demanded was modest, but not small, and the case itself not complex, Lord Woolf proposed a 'fast-track' procedure where time and costs would be rigidly controlled. Other cases would follow the 'multi-track' procedure where the pretrial proceedings would also be strictly controlled. As regards this last category, Lord Woolf thought that it would be restricted just to certain types of case of public importance or (and) where a question of law needed to be tested; the category would also apply to medical compensation claims and cases where there is a right to a jury (defamation).

These reforms proposed by Lord Woolf were welcomed by the government and put into effect by the Civil Procedure Act 1997. A new code of procedural rules was produced whose philosophy is to ensure that the system of justice will be accessible, efficient and fair. Accordingly the first rule of the new Civil Procedure Rules 1998 (CPR) states that a case should be administered above all in a way that is fair.

2.4   NEW PROCEDURAL PHILOSOPHY

What Lord Woolf underlined as the general principle was that the new procedure should ensure equality between the parties together with greater certainty as to costs. The aim is to provide a system of procedure that will prevent a powerful party from acting in an oppressive and unreasonable manner. One way of achieving this would appear to be the importation into the English common law of the idea that a judge should have a role beyond that of presiding over the actual trial; the pretrial proceeding should equally be under the control of the judge, something that happens in many civilian systems. In short, there should be a level playing field and the whole process should, perhaps, not become, as Bracton once thought, like a game of chess. One might note, also, that the Human Rights Act 1998 reinforces this philosophy in as much as Article 6 of the European Convention on Human Rights guarantees as a constitutional right proper access to the justice system.

The effects of these new procedural rules are beginning to be felt in the case law. In *Goode v Martin* ([2002] 1 WLR 1828) the claimant (no longer called 'plaintiff' thanks to the new rules), who was suing for damages for injuries suffered in an accident involving a boat owned by the defendant, wanted to modify her statement of claim (formerly called 'pleadings'). The first instance judge refused this modification on the ground that rule 17 of the CPR 1998 seemed to prohibit any such change except in regard to the 'same facts' set out in the statement, the judge concluding that the claimant was actually trying to modify the statement of facts. The Court of

Appeal allowed an appeal on the basis both of the first rule in the CPR and of s 3(1) of the Human Rights Act 1998, this latter section encouraging a court to interpret a legislative provision in such a manner that it conforms to the European Convention on Human Rights (see 4.9–4.11). According to the appeal court it would be unfair to refuse a modification because such a refusal would entail a new legal action which would obviously increase the costs and delay to the claimant.

What is interesting about this decision is that, when compared to a decision given half a century earlier, it is seemingly indicating a change of attitude. In *Esso Petroleum v Southport Corporation* ([1956] AC 218) the House of Lords had refused to allow a claimant to alter its pleadings and add a new cause of action – even although the facts themselves seemed to indicate liability under the proposed new cause of action – on the basis that conforming to the strict rules of procedure would render better justice than being sympathetic to the claimants' substantive rights. The claimant had failed to assert in its pleadings that the defendants owed it a direct (rather than vicarious) duty of care and it was now too late for the claimant to alter the claim. There was probably no clear formal rule preventing such a modification to the pleadings – for according to the Judicature Acts the claimant was probably under an obligation only to state the facts – and thus the reason why the judges took such a formal approach was to be found in the prevailing philosophy of the time. Despite the abolition of the forms of action a century earlier, the attitude that justice was as much a formal process – a game of 'chess' where the right category or categories of liability had to be set out from the beginning so that a defendant need formally answer only these assertions – was still embedded in the common law mentality. Whether Lord Woolf has fully succeeded in reorientating, in the long term, the English common law towards a new procedural philosophy no doubt remains to be seen.

Finally with respect to procedural philosophy, mention should perhaps be made of the tribunal system (see 1.12) because the procedural philosophy, even before the reform of 2007, was always different from the one associated with traditional civil procedure. An essential characteristic of a tribunal was the more informal procedural structure and the active roles of the tribunal judges; in other words the tribunals were much less adversarial and this perhaps was one reason for their success. Now that the tribunals have been seemingly elevated into an alternative two-tier court system – and even perhaps into a separate administrative courts regime – it may be that at the level of procedural philosophy a distinction can be made between public and private law procedure. Such a distinction would no doubt be inapplicable to the regime of judicial review and the Administrative Court (a Divisional Court of the QBD), but in terms of statistics many more disputes are dealt with by tribunals than by the Administrative Court.

2.5   MODERN APPEAL SYSTEM

Another fundamental motivation underpinning these procedural reforms is the desire to reduce the burden of work on the judges in the Court of Appeal. The new rules are thus designed to deflect the less important appeal work away from this court. To achieve this, a new structure has been put in place in which appeals depend upon the hierarchy of judges. In the civil process an appeal is from one judge to a judge who is immediately superior in the hierarchy and so in principle a case goes from a circuit judge (county court) to a judge in the High Court, although in multi-track cases it would normally still go to the Court of Appeal irrespective of the status of the trial judge. The possibility of a second appeal from a High Court judge to the Court of Appeal still exists, but it will be rare and restricted to cases which give rise to an important point of law or indicate other compelling reasons (*Tanfern Ltd v Cameron-MacDonald (Practice Note)* [2000] 1 WLR 1102). The important development that needs to be stressed here is that there is not an automatic right to go to the Court of Appeal, although there are several exceptions; permission of this court has to be obtained.

Before 1998 an appeal to the Court of Appeal involved a 'rehearing' and while this did not mean that the witnesses were reheard (or a jury reconvened) it did mean that the court could make decisions with respect to both fact and law (*Viscount de L'Isle v Times Newspapers* [1988] 1 WLR 49, 62). In other words it was an 'appeal' and not a *cassation* in the French sense (decision only on a question of law: see below 2.8). The whole case itself was reviewed on the basis of the documents (witness statements and the like). The reforms have seemingly changed the orientation from a rehearing to a 'review' where the emphasis is now on the judgment of the trial judge and this raises the question of whether the process has shifted more towards the continental model of a review (*cassation*) rather than a rehearing of the whole case. In fact it is not clear whether this is a fundamental change since it would be an exaggeration to think that there was ever a clear line between the two notions. However, what one can say is that the Court of Appeal will allow an appeal only where the judge was in error or where there has been a procedural injustice.

As we have seen, a further appeal to the House of Lords was retained in 1875 – and put onto a statutory basis a year later (Appellate Jurisdiction Act 1876) – and so the possibility exists that a case will not end with a decision in the Court of Appeal. However, this third tier was always something of a constitutional anomaly because the Law Lords, as members of the House of Lords, were part of a political institution involved with legislation and this violated the principle of the separation of powers, in turn violating the European Convention on Human Rights, Article 6. Despite the long history of the House of Lords as a legal institution, the government felt that this position could no longer be maintained and this third tier has now become the Supreme Court (Constitutional Reform Act 2005) (for a summary of the debates see Darbyshire, 2011, 158–166).

However, access to this third tier is strictly controlled in that permission to appeal must be obtained either from the Court of Appeal or from the Supreme Court itself. The latter procedure is by way of petition which is considered normally by a team of three Supreme Court justices who will allow or reject the petition without giving reasons. The Supreme Court has inherited the jurisdiction of the old House of Lords, which in turn had the same jurisdiction as the Court of Appeal; it thus is a genuine appeal court rather than one which strictly reviews the application of the law by the inferior judges. In practice, however, the case must normally raise a point of law of public importance.

2.6   ROLE OF AN APPEAL JUDGE

What is the role of an appeal judge? Or, put another way, is the role rather different from that of the trial judge? If one starts with the trial judge, this has been described in the following way:

> The function of a judge of first instance is to find the relevant facts and, with the assistance of counsel, to ascertain the law as set out in any relevant statutory provisions and in principles to be derived from the decisions of the House of Lords and the Court of Appeal, and to draw the appropriate legal consequences. It is not open to the judge in performing this primary function to consider, far less express an opinion, as to the correctness of a decision of the Court of Appeal or the House of Lords except in those rare cases where he is faced with conflicting decisions of the Court of Appeal and must choose which to follow.

As Vinelott J went on to say:

> That does not rest solely upon the feelings of deference and respect which a judge of first instance will naturally and properly approach a decision of the Court of Appeal or the House of Lords. An opinion which the judge may entertain as to the correctness or otherwise of, for instance, the interpretation of a decision of the House of Lords by the Court of Appeal, is simply irrelevant to

his primary duty which is to ascertain the statutory provisions and the principles stated in decisions that are binding on him which govern the case before him (*Derby & Co v Weldon (No. 5)* [1989] 1 WLR 1244, 1250)

There are a number of ways in which an appeal judgment is now subtly different from a first instance one. Although an appeal court traditionally hears appeals on both questions of fact and questions of law, such a court is always reluctant to interfere with the findings of fact made by a first instance judge who has heard and seen the witnesses (*Watt v Thomas* [1947] AC 484). Jury verdicts are even more difficult, for juries do not give reasons and a verdict cannot normally be quashed simply on the ground of unreasonableness (*Grobbelaar v News Group Newspapers Ltd* [2002] 1 WLR 3024). Moreover, as we have seen, under the new procedural rules an appeal is no longer by way of 'rehearing' but by way of 'review'; this suggests that there has been a shift of emphasis from the case itself to the appealed judgment under review. This said, the Court of Appeal has recently indicated that in practice not all that much has changed (*Assicurazoni Generali SpA v Arab Insurance Group* [2003] 1 WLR 577).

Another reason for the difference between a first instance and appeal judgment is that appeal judgments have a more central role in the precedent system. Thus, according to Lord Diplock: 'In a judgment, particularly one that has not been reduced into writing before delivery, a judge, whether at first instance or upon appeal, has his mind concentrated upon the particular facts of the case before him and the course which the oral argument has taken.' Yet even when a case comes before the Court of Appeal this factual dimension must not be lost from view. Lord Diplock thus continued:

> The primary duty of the Court of Appeal on an appeal in any case is to determine the matter actually in dispute between the parties. Such propositions of law as members of the court find necessary to state and previous authorities to which they find it convenient to refer in order to justify the disposition of the actual proceedings before them will be tailored to the facts of the particular case. Accordingly, propositions of law may well be stated in terms either more general or more specific than would have been used if he who gave the judgment had in mind somewhat different facts, or had heard a legal argument more expansive than had been necessary in order to determine the particular appeal.

And he went on to add:

> Even when making successive revisions of drafts of my own written speeches for delivery upon appeals to this House, which usually involve principles of law of wider application than the particular case under appeal, I often find it necessary to continue to introduce subordinate clauses supplementing, or qualifying, the

simpler, and stylistically preferable, wording in which statements of law have been expressed in earlier drafts (*Roberts Petroleum Ltd v Bernard Kenny Ltd* [1983] 2 AC 192, 201).

The role of an appeal judge is not, therefore, to assert general principles of law or even general legal rules. It is to fashion a proposition that fits the material facts of the case in hand. All the same it has to be asked whether Lord Diplock's observations always provide an accurate picture for all appeal cases. Certainly, as we shall see (Chapter 4), the facts are vital. Yet there are judgments that can lay down very general principles, perhaps the most famous being Lord Atkin's 'neighbour principle' in *Donoghue v Stevenson* ([1932] AC 562).

2.7 COLLEGIALITY

With respect to the appeal judgment itself, the tradition that each judge has the right to issue his or her own opinion continues to be the rule. However, in practice the Court of Appeal is tending towards issuing a single judgment of the court itself, a practice that has been criticised both by academics (Munday, 2002) and by Lord Denning (*The Hannah Blumenthal* [1983] 1 AC 854, 873–874). Such a development suggests, again, a shift towards the continental model: the individualism of the common law judge is giving way to the collegiality of the court. However, whatever may be the position with regard to the Court of Appeal, the tradition of independent judgments continues in the Supreme Court. Moreover, it is unlikely that collegiality in the civilian sense of the term will ever become a characteristic of common law procedure since the institution of the dissenting judgment is firmly entrenched in the common law tradition (Kirby, 2007).

Nevertheless it would be wrong to dismiss from English law the whole idea of collegiality because it can exist in some weaker forms. In particular the relation between counsel and judges is a close one not just outside of the courts where judges mix professionally and socially with barristers in the Inns of Court, but within the court process as well. The judges rely on counsel to research and to present to them the law, their arguments being tested during the oral debate. In the appeal courts such presentation and argumentation can sometimes seem like an academic seminar with the result that it is not empirically true to say that it is the judges who make the common law. It is in reality a joint effort between barristers and judges and one could say that there is here a kind of professional collegiality, especially in a system where judges are chosen from these practitioners (see further Samuel, 2011).

Becoming a High Court (and later an appeal) judge in England is not traditionally a profession one chooses after graduating or qualifying and thus one where collegiality is perhaps something of a formal necessity in order to help preserve the bureaucratic nature of applying the law. It is a profession that one might join after many years of practice within a social group that has its own loose kind of collegiality in and around the Inns of Court (which were once colleges). One must also remember that in the early days of the common law there were not many judges, barely into double figures, and so historically one can certainly say there was a corps or 'college' of judges. Today there are many more, but if one focuses just on the senior courts, not as many as in many other European countries' senior courts. However, as John Bell notes, things are perhaps changing; a career pattern is beginning to emerge and the number of judges is increasing substantially (Bell, 2006). It is becoming more and more unrealistic to regard judging as a 'cottage industry' in England (Bell, 2006, 346).

2.8   COMPARATIVE EXCURSUS: *PROCÈS*, TRIAL, APPEAL, *RENVOI* AND *CASSATION*

If one had to choose one single difference between civilian and common law procedure it is, perhaps, to be found in the absence of any idea on the Continent of a trial. By 'trial' is meant the notion of a 'day in court' (or series of days) where all the evidence is presented, originally to a jury, witnesses are cross-examined, and the legal arguments are made to the judge, the judge and jury (if there is one) reaching their decisions at the end of these presentations. In other words a trial is a condensed event developed because jurymen had only a limited time period in which they could be away from their normal employment and judges, on circuit from London, had to deal with many cases in each location. The civilian 'process', by contrast, is a much more drawn out event divided up into various stages. In many ways it is more of an inquiry in which the claims and evidence are reduced to a dossier and judgment is given on the contents of this dossier (this is an exaggeration but not much of one).

Another important difference, arising out of the distinction between trial and process, is the role of the judge. In continental procedure the judge has a more active role extending over all stages of the process; in English procedure, until 1998 at least, the role of the judge was limited to the trial stage and even here his or her role remained passive as compared to the role of a judge on the Continent (although there are exceptions). It is these differences which have given rise to the labels 'inquisitorial' and 'accusatorial' (or adversarial) being applied to civilian and common law procedure respectively.

Judgment rendered in proceedings at first instance may not mark the end of litigation since in all Western legal systems there is the possibility, if not the right, of appeal. In addition there may be some further possibility of review, if not appeal, from a decision given by the appeal court. Such possibilities assume the existence of a judicial hierarchy – or perhaps pyramid would be a more appropriate metaphor (Herzog & Karlen) – in which there are many courts of first instance forming the base of the pyramid. Above these first instance courts there are courts of appeal which, in the French model in particular, are regionalised. At this level the pyramid is narrower because there are fewer such appeal courts in comparison with first instance ones. Finally there is a single court at the top of the pyramid whose sole function is to review the judgments coming from the appeal courts.

In France, both appeal and review come under the single expression *les voies de recours*. An appeal is where a party asks a tribunal higher up in the pyramid (*cour d'appel*) to judge the case a second time and is justified by the idea that judges can be fallible. It assumes, of course, that the judges in the higher court are more competent and experienced. One particular point that needs to be made about an 'appeal' is that it is virtually a second 'process' in that the court can adjudicate on both fact and law (*Code de procédure civile* (CPC) art 561). However such an appeal will in general be governed by the principles *tantum devolutem quantum appellatum* and *tantum devolutem quantum judicatum*: only the litigation judged at first instance can be transported before an appeal court and thus new facts and new points of law cannot in theory be raised (CPC art 561). In practice this rule is subject to certain exceptions (see, for example, CPC art 563).

In England there is only one Court of Appeal in London with a further appeal to the Supreme Court, also in London. In civil law systems, in contrast, the administration of justice tends to be decentralised, even with respect to appeal courts. Thus in France there is not a single *cour d'appel* situated in the capital; there are regional appeal courts situated in various major towns. In Germany each *Land* has its own appeal structure; there are regional courts which hear some appeals and now higher regional courts acting as final courts of appeal in many cases.

There may also be a reference to a constitutional court if, in any case, a constitutional question emerges from the litigation. Until recently such a reference was impossible in France; however in 2008 the French constitution was changed and thus 'when, during the course of a case before a court, it is argued that a legislative provision invades the rights and liberties that the Constitution guarantees, the matter can be submitted to the *Conseil constitutionnel* by way of a reference (*renvoi*) from the *Conseil d'État* or from the *Cour de cassation* which will decide within a fixed time limit' (art 61-1 of the constitution). Such a reference will not, it must be stressed, decide the actual litigation in issue; that is a question for the civil court. The constitutional court will give a ruling only with regard to the constitutional rights issue.

There is no separate constitutional court in the United Kingdom and so any issues of constitutional law will be decided by the ordinary courts. However, with respect to European Union law there is a reference procedure from the English courts to the European Court of Justice (Treaty on the Functioning of the European Union Art 267). This is a reference (*renvoi*) and not an appeal because the European Court cannot decide the case itself; it can only give a ruling on the interpretation of European Community law. The role of the European Court is to ensure the uniform interpretation throughout the European Union of community law. This idea of a reference procedure is now becoming more established internally in the UK and thus although the UK does not have a constitutional court independent from a supreme court the latter can be described as having a constitutional function.

This role of the European Court is in some ways similar to that of the French *Cour de cassation* whose role is to ensure the uniform interpretation and application of legislation in France (Perrot, 2010, 266). Accordingly the appeal courts in France – and in Germany – are not at the peak of the pyramid. In Germany there is the possibility of a further 'appeal' to a third (federal) level in the hierarchy. However these are not appeals as such, but revision in that the court is not re-judging the case but reviewing the judgments of the appeal court. Consequently if one had to choose one institution that perhaps typifies, if in rather an extreme way, this third level of jurisdiction, it would be the French *Cour de cassation*, which has served as something of a model in the civilian world (see Watkin, 1997, 105–106). It was established (largely on the ruins of the old *Parlement de Paris*?) after the Revolution to ensure the uniform application of the *Code civil* in France. Thus its role is *not* that of an appeal court; its role is to review the way a lower court has applied the code and thus the object of its attention is not the litigation as such but the judgment of the *Cour d'appel*.

There is only one *Cour de cassation*, situated in Paris, and its scope of action is procedurally limited: it can in principle do only one of two things. It can reject a *pourvoi en cassation*, thus allowing the judgment of the *Cour d'appel* to stand, or it can quash (*casser*) a decision. If it does the latter it cannot, in principle, substitute its own decision; it has to send the case back to a different *Cour d'appel* from the one from which the case emanated. However, what if the *Cour d'appel* to which the case is sent arrives at the same (quashed) decision as the original appeal court? In this situation a second *pourvoi en cassation* comes before a plenary session (*Assemblée plénière*) of the court and if it quashes the decision it will be sent to yet another *Cour d'appel* which will be bound by the *Cour de cassation*'s interpretation of the law. The court is now divided into six chambers; and there is also a new procedure whereby the court can give an advisory opinion and in certain cases make its own decisions.

One can see therefore that, despite the three-tied court structure in England and in France, the Supreme Court and the *Cour de cassation* are rather different institutions. Indeed some even argue that the *Cour de cassation* is not actually a 'court' but an institution that oversees the interpretation and application of legislation. In other words, it is a legislative body rather than a court. However many of the judges in this institution would probably not agree with this assessment. Whatever the situation, the United Kingdom Supreme Court is not a review court as such but an appeal court which can render its own decisions. It can therefore decide issues that would formerly have been decided by a jury (see e.g. *Bolton v Stone* [1951] AC 850). However, this said, the Supreme Court hears only around 80 or 90 cases a year (maybe fewer) whereas the *Cour de cassation* deals with over 25,000 cases every year. Another difference is to be found in the style and structure of the judgments issuing from the two systems. In the case of all English courts the judgments are usually individualised and very discursive (see above 2.6). In contrast, the *Cour de cassation* renders only one short and terse judgment set out in the form of a syllogism. In order to appreciate the substantive reasons as to why the French court has decided the way it has the researcher will need to examine the reports of both the *juge rapporteur* and Advocate-General plus the academic commentary in the law journals (Lasser, 2004).

2.9   COMMON PROCEDURAL PRINCIPLES?

One characteristic that has emerged from the comparisons so far is that the Romano-canonical model is said to be inquisitorial while the common law adheres to an accusatorial or adversarial procedure. The accusatorial procedure is normally characterised as being public, oral and contradictory (which means that the accused is free to rebut during the trial the arguments raised against him by the accuser); whereas the inquisitorial is secret, written and non-contradictory (which means that the accused will be able to defend himself only at a certain moment in the process) (Stein,

1984, 36–38). In fact the labels are misleading since the civilian process now has an accusatorial dimension and there are aspects of English law that seem more inquisitorial than adversary (family law cases involving children for example). As for secrecy, English judges and politicians are probably in no position any longer to lecture other nations. This said, both in the French and the German models there are certain general principles to be found in the codes of procedure which act as foundational starting points for the modern process. In Germany civil procedure is regulated by the *Zivilprozeßordnung* (ZPO) and in France by the CPC. Are these principles really any different from those that underpin the procedural philosophy of the common law?

The first principle is a requirement, on the part of the parties, of a legitimate interest in the proceedings. It is probably true to say that it is a general principle throughout the civil law that only those persons who have a legitimate interest in a case can be a party to proceedings (*pas d'intérêt, pas d'action*). This rule is quite specific in French law where only those with such an interest can bring or defend an action (CPC art 31). In English law there is such a requirement in respect of a judicial review action (see 3.12), but there does not seem to be a specific procedural rule requiring such an interest in private law claims. However, the reason for this absence is that the substantive law which lies behind most common law remedies will itself preclude those without a sufficient interest from bringing a claim. Thus an action in negligence requires a duty of care to exist between the parties and in most tort and contract claims there is a requirement that the victim suffers damage. For example, in a claim for public nuisance or breach of statutory duty the claimant must be able to show special damage over and above the damage suffered by the public in general. This interest, or standing, question has become particularly acute when 'more and more frequently the complexity of modern societies generates situations in which a single human action can be beneficial or prejudicial to large numbers of people, thus making entirely inadequate the traditional scheme of litigation as merely a two-party affair' (Cappelletti, 1989, 271). A commercial organisation pollutes the environment: who has standing to sue? A seller hugely profits by committing a fraud on his customers but each individual customer suffers only a minute loss: does this mean no one can sue for lack of a sufficient interest? These are important access-to-justice questions which affect both the civil and the common law.

A second overriding principle to be found in civilian procedure is that civil proceedings are subject to party control (*Judex secundum allegata et probata partium judicare debet*). Thus the French procedural code states in its first article that except where the law provides otherwise, only the parties can institute proceedings (*l'instance*). And they are free to put an end to the proceedings before they are extinguished by the effect of judgment or by law. A similar principle is to be found in German law. It should be noted, however, that once a case is before a judge, the latter is usually required to make a decision independently of any initiative taken by the parties (see, for example, CPC arts 7, 12). What the judge must not do is to make a decision *ultra petita* (see, for example, CPC art 7). This parties principle is undoubtedly true of English law as well since it is an essential characteristic of the accusatorial model.

Thirdly, there is now a principle of orality in the civil law and so despite the fundamental importance of the dossier in Romano-canonical, and in modern, continental civil procedure, the right to an oral hearing has become a basic procedural principle. Parties must have the right to present facts, evidence and legal arguments orally in court. However, in practice this right does not seem to be that important, partly because there is not a legal tradition of cross-examination of witnesses in public in front of a jury. Indeed in France hearings before the full court are brief and it is not common for lawyers to present their arguments of law orally. The *dossier* remains the basis of French procedure and in Germany written presentation and written documentation is the norm. In English law the principle of orality has receded to some extent, especially with respect to appeal proceedings (Zander, 2007, 682–685). Since 1983 there has been a requirement that counsel should provide to the Court of Appeal a written document briefly setting out the arguments that they intend to use (Practice Direction [1983] 2 All ER 34) and this requirement followed a similar development with regard to the House of Lords (now Supreme Court). Today these skeleton arguments are now an important part of the civil process, but, this said, the judges still see oral argument as a central feature of the litigation process (*Khader v Aziz* [2010] 1 WLR 2673, paras 37, 52 ; *Moore v BWB* [2013] 3 WLR 43, paras 48–51).

Fourthly, proceedings are subject to the principle of contradiction. This principle is basically a translation into a procedural rule of the maxim *audi alteram partem* (hear the other side) and so, for example, the French procedural code specifically states that judgment shall not be given against a party who has not been summoned (CPC art 14) and that the 'parties must inform each other within a reasonable time of the grounds of fact on which they base their claims or defences, the evidence that they adduce and the legal grounds they invoke, so that each can be in a position to organise his claims and defences' (CPC art 15). If the judge bases his decision on legal grounds that he has raised *ex officio*, he can only do this 'if he has first invited the parties to give their observations' (art 16). A similar principle is found in German civil procedure and the maxim *audi alteram partem* has central importance not just in English procedural law but equally in English substantive administrative law. Judges are normally very reluctant to rule on any matter that has not been properly argued before them.

Finally, there is the principle of publicity: as a general rule all hearings are in public although there are exceptions. The French procedural code accordingly states that the 'hearings are in public, except in cases where the law requires or permits that they take place in camera' (art 22). Once again there is no doubt that this maxim applies equally to the English common law (CPR r 39.2(1)), but as the French rule indicates it is often rather meaningless in its scope in that the second half of the rules goes far in negating the first half. The law is able to require that proceedings take place in secret (CPR r 39.2(3)). In fact the situation turns out to be complex in English law because although there are now situations where proceedings are indeed held in camera there are also a range of intermediate situations. Thus there are powers for the courts to restrict the reporting of cases (see Contempt of Court Act 1981, s 11), even if under the European Convention on Human Rights (Art 10) this restriction must be balanced against the right of freedom of expression.

There has also been successful pressure from the security services to institute closed civil proceedings. Such a secret ('closed') civil procedure is to be used in situations where 'a party to the proceedings would be required to disclose sensitive material in the course of the proceedings to another person (whether or not another party to the proceedings)' (Justice and Security Act 2013 s 6(4)). The effect of this new law will be to exclude the claimant and his or her lawyer from the proceedings and thus the case will be decided entirely behind closed doors, the claimant himself and his lawyer not having the chance to examine, or cross-examine, the defendant's evidence. The claimant's interest is represented only by a 'special advocate' (s 9). One result of this new procedure is, seemingly, to convert the process from a genuine adversarial model to one that is more inquisitorial in orientation in that it will consist largely of a secret inquiry involving the party wishing to plead sensitive material (normally a public authority or agent), the judge and a specially vetted advocate supposedly representing the interests of the excluded party. Given that the specially vetted advocate will have been chosen by the state, and that one party might never know the substantive reason(s) for the dismissal of his or her case, one wonders whether this procedure amounts to a fair trial according to Article 6 of the Convention for the Protection of Human Rights and Fundamental Freedoms. Whatever the situation, it is not just that open justice is becoming less important in the English common law; civil procedure itself is beginning to display signs of a public and private divide with the result that actions against public authorities will probably be increasingly governed by special procedural principles.

2.10   LEGAL SERVICES

In addition to legal procedure itself, mention needs to be made of what might be called legal services in general, for very, very few legal issues and disputes ever reach the courts. This raises the question of what lies between a legal dispute and access to the courts, and the answer is a range of legal, quasi-legal and non-legal services. These services are provided by people and institutions which, in recent years, have become much more diverse as a result of quite fundamental changes in the structure of the legal professions and the funding of litigation.

The starting point is the legal profession or, more precisely in England, the legal professions. In England and Wales this group of legal professionals has been divided into two, each of which enjoyed monopolies during the 20th century. Barristers as a legal profession have a long history associated with the Inns of Court which date back to the end of the 13th century. A century later there were four such Inns – Gray's Inn, Lincoln's Inn, Inner Temple and Middle Temple – and during the 17th century only members of these Inns could practise in the common law courts. These practitioners were professional advocates who not only acted as the intermediaries between litigants and judges but became the specialists of procedure and substantive law with the result that the tradition developed of appointing judges only from these advocates. During the 19th century the rule emerged that barristers could not be hired directly by a litigant but had to be appointed by a solicitor.

This second group of professionals grew out of the rather diverse history of English practitioners in as much as there existed by the 17th century various categories of professionals, one of which was the class of 'solicitors' who solicited clients by helping them through the procedural complexities of the law. At first there was no clear distinction between barristers and solicitors but gradually a division of functions led to a separation, with the solicitors becoming a fully professional body with the establishment of the Law Society in the 19th century. This professional body was subsequently confirmed by statute (Supreme Court of Judicature Act 1873, s 87).

The monopolies enjoyed by the profession during the last century were court representation for barristers (advocacy) and conveyancing (sale and transfer of title in land) for solicitors. These two areas of work still define the essence of being a barrister and a solicitor, although the scope of work for solicitors has always been very much wider than just dealing with the transfer of real property. Generally speaking, solicitors were the professionals in control of the pretrial proceedings while barristers handled the trial stage. Solicitors also offered general legal advice and service – they are sometimes compared with the general practitioner (GPs) in the medical profession – and, with the growth of the large city practices, this advice became more and more specialised. It is the solicitors' firms that are now the experts on large areas of commercial and international commercial law. Barristers, as well as being advocates, were equally often specialists in particular areas of law and thus were often hired by solicitors to provide counsel's opinion on a point of law for a client. If one continues the medical analogy, barristers were and are sometimes regarded as the specialist consultants. This pattern of work has not changed that much, although the growth of large city firms of solicitors has rendered the medical analogy a little obsolete. However the laws that enshrined the pattern as monopolies has changed with the result that the 21st century may turn out to look rather different from a legal services point of view than the previous century.

The Conservative government that came to power in 1979 was largely in favour of economic liberalism and thus had a distrust of all monopolies, which they regarded as anti-competitive. Both the court representation and the conveyancing monopolies were progressively loosened (Courts and Legal Services Act 1990; Access to Justice Act 1999) and the regulation of each profession has also been subject to quite dramatic change. The professions are now supervised by an independent board (Legal Services Act 2007). In addition the traditional business structures have been subject to reform. Barristers cannot form partnerships and so operate as individual contractors working in groups known as chambers, traditionally within an Inn of Court. Solicitors can form partnerships – even limited liability ones – but now there is the opportunity to create licensed alternative business structures in which other non-law firms can invest (Legal Services Act 2007). There is the possibility that household banking and supermarket institutions might open law centres within their own premises and this new development has attracted the name 'Tesco law' (after the large supermarket called Tesco). Developments are at an early stage and these new structures are not without their critics. Is the provision of legal services to be regarded as no different from the provision of baked beans? Even if law services are different from other services, there is no doubt that many regard the service provided by English professionals as governed by market forces. The large city firms of solicitors now have a major international presence and can be seen as, amongst other things, selling English law as a commodity.

2.11   FINANCING LEGAL SERVICES

These alternative business structures will no doubt provide a high-quality service to the commercial community. But what about the other classes? What about the ordinary people of limited, sometimes very limited, financial means? Here the situation is more complex. Various models of funding are possible. At one extreme of course there is the neoliberal model in which financing is left entirely to the market and if this results in exclusion of a large class of persons so be it. Law is simply no different than a luxury hotel: it is open to all who can afford it. However, this model attracts to two serious criticisms. The first is that law is not like a luxury hotel; it is a fundamental social institution founded upon the idea that all are equal before the law and thus nobody should be excluded from its services on the ground of economic circumstances. A second, and linked, criticism is that equal access is seemingly guaranteed as a human right under Article 6 of the European Convention on Human Rights. It is arguable that the state is obliged to ensure such access.

How can such access be achieved? If one moves from the neoliberal model to the other extreme, the state could provide legal aid to all those who cannot afford access themselves. At this extreme the cost would be demand led; that is to say legal aid would be available to fund any litigant without means who wanted to pursue a reasonable case. England went far in establishing such a scheme with the Legal Aid and Advice Act 1949. However, as Lord Bingham in a brief but informative survey indicated, this model encountered problems in respect both of its huge cost and of the classes that it excluded. It served the poorest well, but not those of modest means (*Callery v Gray* [2001] 1 WLR 2112, para 1). This led to a change of model; a scheme was introduced that shifted the focus off funding litigation to funding service providers by way of contract between a Legal Aid Board and firms of solicitors. When this also proved unsatisfactory in respect of personal injury claims the government moved to a model whereby the cost was placed on the service providers themselves, including insurance companies (Access to Justice Act 1999). This was achieved through the conditional fee agreement and insurance whereby the solicitor firm of the successful party can claim not just its costs but an uplift fee (Lord Bingham in *Callery v Gray*, paras 2–6; see also Lord Hope paras 47–54). The government has now restricted to an absolute minimum state-provided legal aid (Legal Aid, Sentencing and Punishment of Offenders Act 2012); the model will thus be one where access to justice is to be facilitated only through schemes provided by the legal service providers and litigants themselves. In other words the move is towards a neoliberal model.

The provision of financial legal aid to poor litigants is not the only method through which legal services can be financed. Reducing the costs of legal services and litigation is another method and so the recent legal aid reforms have to be viewed in the context of the reform of civil procedure (see 2.3) and of business structures (see 2.10). In addition the legal service providers, and other institutions, can offer schemes such as free advice and low cost aid to the less well off. In addition one must not forget that litigants themselves are not legally obliged to employ solicitors and barristers; they can act as litigants in person often with the aid of a friend (*McKenzie v McKenzie* [1970] 3 All ER 1034).

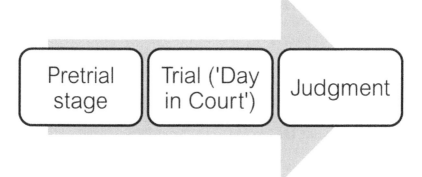

Figure 2.1   Trial

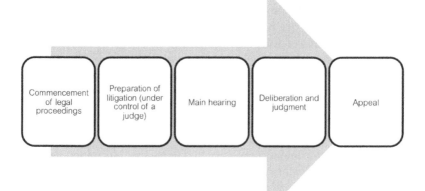

Figure 2.2   Procès

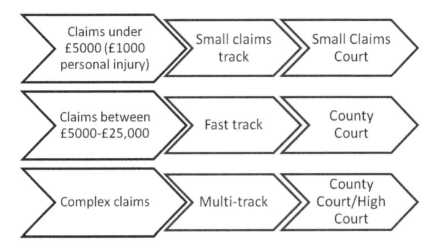

Figure 2.3   Procedural tracks (following Woolf Report)

3. English law remedies

Merely examining the courts and the civil procedure in England does not give the full picture of the spirit and mentality of the common law tradition. Even at the level of the law of actions more needs to be said about the important institutional role of legal remedies since they still have an important active force. In the civilian tradition the dichotomy is largely one between procedure and substantive law, but in England the legal remedy lies midway between civil procedure and substantive law and this is one of the distinctive features of the common law tradition. Textbooks have been written on legal remedies (see, for example, Lawson, 1980).

Given the long history of the forms of action, perhaps the most suitable focal point for a practical understanding of English law is, then, that of the legal *actio* or remedy. We have seen that the history of English law is largely a history of actions each of which, originally, had its own procedural form. This law of actions emphasis is equally true of the Court of Chancery which developed its own substantive law ideas through the use of new, largely non-monetary, remedies. The emphasis on remedies is still a distinctive feature of English law (see, for example, Zakrzewski, 2005) and it is therefore of the utmost importance, when reading ('briefing') a case from a common law jurisdiction, to identify at the start the remedy in issue. However, modern remedies, and causes of action (see Chapters 6–7), can properly be understood only after an examination of their historical foundations.

3.1 PERSONAL ACTIONS AT COMMON LAW

All legal claims, including the claim that a jury verdict or court judgment was erroneous, were once started via a real or a personal action, each of which was based directly or indirectly on a writ (see 1.6). These actions determined not just the claimant's 'right' but also the procedure to be followed. Choosing the wrong action (writ) could be fatal to the claim, the claimant (plaintiff) having to recommence using a different action. Many, but not all, of the original actions have now disappeared from view, either because they have been eclipsed by more recent causes of action or because they have been suppressed, but others still survive as remedies or as causes of action. One should perhaps add that before the 19th century the idea of an appeal against a judgment could be seen in terms of a remedy; the disappointed litigant would seek redress through a Writ of Error, in origin an original writ like trespass (that is to say issuing out of the office of the Lord Chancellor representing the king's legal interests).

The main formal distinction to be found in the early days of the common law was the one between real and personal actions. Real actions were those brought for the specific recovery of land, tenements or hereditaments, whereas personal actions were those brought for the specific recovery of moveable goods, of a debt, of damages or for other redress. By the end of the 14th century real actions had largely fallen into disuse as a result not just of the decline of feudalism but also of unpopularity owing to their excessive procedural technicalities. The history of common law remedies is, therefore, largely a history of personal actions. In the early days of the common law courts, the court which supposedly had exclusive jurisdiction over personal actions was the Court of Common Pleas. However this arrangement

> was departed from at the expense of the Court of Common Pleas, for the other two courts, while retaining each its own exclusive jurisdiction, succeeded in encroaching upon the jurisdiction of the Common Pleas over personal actions, with the result that in modern times any personal action could be brought in any one of the three Courts of Common Law (Sutton, 1929, 36).

3.2 TYPES OF PERSONAL ACTION

The personal actions at common law were very different from the *actiones* to be found in Roman law and were based on the system of writs. The original formulation of each action was a response to an empirical problem that existed in English society at the time of formulation. However, some of the actions subsequently became enlarged, if not deformed, through development by lawyers and courts, often through the use of fictions. The main actions which were to survive into the 19th century (if not later) are the following (discussed alphabetically).

The action of *account* was a writ ordering the defendant to render an account of the plaintiff's money. The action was less an actual claim than an accounting process aimed at identifying money in the defendant's possession 'belonging' to the plaintiff. Account 'was not therefore primarily concerned with the obligation to pay [a] sum, which sounded in debt, but with the antecedent obligation to enter into an account in order to discover what, if anything, was owing' (Baker, 2002, 363). By the 16th century the common law action for an account had declined into oblivion, but in form the remedy survived in the Court of Chancery and by the 19th century account was regarded as an equitable, rather than common law, remedy (see *London, Chatham & Dover Railway Co v S.E. Railway Co* [1892] 1 Ch 120, 140).

The action of *assumpsit* was a development of trespass on the case (see below) and was used as a means of claiming damages for a breach of promise. Viewed from a modern perspective, it can be seen as the remedial basis for a theory of contractual liability (see 7.2). The Court of King's Bench developed a particular type of *assumpsit* so as to be able to attract debt claims which were normally brought in Common Pleas. Thus two types of *assumpsit* were established: there was the general action for damages for damage arising from an unperformed promise and a debt-like claim for the recovery of a specific sum of money (Ibbetson, 1999, 147–151). As both claims were technically for damages, the debt and damages distinction ought, perhaps, to have disappeared. Yet it did not. Indeed the distinction not only survived but a claim in debt is regarded as a different cause of action from a claim in damages (*Overstone Ltd v Shipway* [1962] 1 WLR 117). One might add that in order for *assumpsit* to lie there had to be some kind of *quid pro quo* (reciprocity); this requirement subsequently developed into the doctrine of consideration (Ibbetson, 1999, 142), which in turn became one of the fundamental requirements for an enforceable contract at common law (see 7.3).

Another 'contractual' action was *covenant*, which was a claim for damages arising out of the breach of a 'covenant', that is a promise given under seal. It had several procedural disadvantages and as a result never really developed into a general claim for breach of contract. Yet the action has to some extent survived into the modern world in that a unilateral promise executed as a deed will still be binding (see Law of Property (Miscellaneous Provisions) Act 1989, s 1).

A further action used by a disappointed 'contractor' was the writ of *debt*, which was an action for a specific sum of money alleged to be due to the plaintiff and generally arising out of some 'contract' between the parties. This action was one of the oldest in the common law and was actually as much a 'property' claim as a contractual one (Ibbetson, 1999, 18). However in the 17th century, as mentioned, debt got eclipsed to a certain extent by the special form of *assumpsit* called *indebitatus assumpsit*, but it nevertheless survived as a separate remedy into the modern law and must therefore be distinguished from an action for damages (*Jervis v Harris* [1996] Ch 195). Indeed the action was not limited to contractual situations and three particular forms of debt developed as restitution (or quasi-contract) remedies. These are the action for money had and received, the action for money paid and the *quantum meruit* action (see Lord Atkin in *United Australia Ltd v Barclays Bank Ltd* [1941] AC 1). These three quasi-contractual debt claims were originally rationalised on the basis that there was an implied contract between the parties, but this theory has now been abandoned. They are now based upon the Roman principle of unjust enrichment (D.50.17.206; Ibbetson, 1999, 284–293) (see 7.5).

If debt was a claim for a specific sum of money, *detinue* was an action for a specific moveable thing. It was accordingly the nearest action that the common law had to an *in rem* claim and was once the remedy used by the owner of a chattel (bailor) who had transferred possession of it to another (bailee) such as a transporter or cleaner (*Building and Civil Engineering Holidays Scheme Management Ltd v Post Office* [1966] 1 QB 247; *Morris v C W Martin & Sons Ltd* [1966] 1 QB 716). The transfer of possession gave rise to a relation called bailment, which was a property relationship independent of any contract between the two parties; the bailee was under a strict duty to return the goods to the bailor and failure to do this would result in liability for damages in detinue, unless the bailee could show that the goods were lost through no fault of his own. Detinue survived as a cause of action in tort until 1977 when it was abolished by statute (Torts (Interference with Goods) Act 1977, s 2(1)). Its role has been taken over by the tort of conversion (1977 Act, s 2(2)).

Another type of property claim was the writ of *ejectment*, which lay where lands or tenements were let for a term of years but the lessee was ejected from the premises. In substance this writ was a real action, but in form it was a personal claim developed by the use of a fiction to avoid the technicalities of an actual real action. The action is still available to anyone, including now a mere contractual licensee, wrongfully dispossessed of land (*Manchester Airport Plc v Dutton* [2000] 1 QB 133).

The Writ of *Error* was a means by which a disappointed litigant could 'appeal' against a court decision on the basis of an error on the face of the record. It was not properly an appeal since the case was never reheard as such; questions of fact or law, a misdirection of the jury, a perverse verdict or whatever could only be considered by a Court of Error if such a basis for 'appeal' formed part of the court record. To make matters worse, there was no proper Court of Error until Parliament established the Court of Exchequer Chamber in 1830. Before then, there had been other Court of Exchequer Chambers and the House of Lords could also act as a final Court of Error; but the system of 'appeal' before 1830 was, to say the least, complex, somewhat haphazard and procedurally narrow and unsatisfactory (the court could only re-examine the record) (see Figure 1.1).

An action for *replevin* lay where goods had been distrained (seized by a creditor) and was the claim by which the owner sought their recovery. However, the most important claim in respect of interference with goods or with the person was the writ of *trespass*. Along with debt, this was another of the common law's oldest writs and is seen as the ultimate source of most of our present-day compensation claims. An action for trespass was in origin a claim for damages against a person who had harmed the plaintiff in breach of the king's peace (*contra pacem nostram*) and by a forcible wrong (*vi et armis*). 'The word "trespass",,' notes Ibbetson, 'meant no more than "wrong", and its legal use had no predetermined boundaries' (1999, 14), but there were three distinct varieties which were to develop, namely trespass to the person (*vi et armis*), to goods (*de bonis asportatis*) and to land (*quare clausum fregit*). These three varieties have survived into the modern law of tort and have an important constitutional and private law status since they are the torts that effectively protect the individual against the state and ensure quiet possession of property.

The writ of trespass subsequently gave rise to an offshoot action called *trespass on the case*, which was a more general form of trespass where the facts did not disclose a forcible wrong and thus fell outside the writ of trespass (direct action). There is some debate over why actions on the case developed, the traditional learning being that when the Register of Writs became closed statute authorised Chancery to issue writs on an analogy with trespass (*in consimili casu*). Whatever the situation, the Action on the Case became the means by which 'trespass' was transformed, from the 14th century onwards, into a more general liability action through the development of 'special cases'. Case thus became both general and particular at the same time in that it consisted of a series of actions based on model special facts, which later developed into particular types of actionable wrongs such as *assumpsit*, *trover*, public nuisance, negligence and so on (see, for example, Denning LJ's judgment in *Esso Petroleum Ltd v Southport Corporation* [1954] 2 QB 182). However, one oddity of case was that trespass and trespass on the case remained independent personal actions whose difference was rationalised, in the 17th century, on the basis of direct (trespass) and indirect (case) damage (see *Scott v Shepherd* (1773) 96 ER 525).

Trover was an action for damages brought against a defendant who had 'converted' to his own use the plaintiff's goods and chattels. It later became known as conversion and is still the main tort for recovering moveable property (Torts (Interference with Goods) Act 1977). As we have seen, conversion can now be used in situations that were once covered only by the tort of detinue; it is the remedy that a bailor uses to recover his goods from a bailee.

3.3 REMEDIES AND CAUSES OF ACTION

The forms of action were abolished by the Common Law Procedure Act 1852 and thus, as Professor van Caenegem has observed, there 'was no need any more to choose one of ca 72 stereotype forms of action (as were still in existence in 1830), each with its own writ and strict formal rules of procedure'. And from then on law suits 'started with a simple uniform writ of summons stating the plaintiff's case, not in any formula put into the king's mouth, but in his own words; the whole course of procedure in an action was no more determined by the first step, that is, the original writ' (1971, para 75). This reform took the emphasis off not just the form of the claim but the actual remedy itself and this is reflected in the legislation dealing with county courts. Actions for 'debt' and 'damages' became actions founded on 'contract' and on 'tort' (see Chapter 7). This in turn put the emphasis on substantive rights and duties with the result that the common law moved towards a new system of classification. Law was no longer a list of remedies, but a law of contract, tort and property (see Chapters 6–7).

However, these new categories were not founded on 'rights' in the sense that the term is used in the civil law. They were categories of causes of action and thus one finds the late-19th-century judges often adopting the Roman law expressions of actions *ex contractu* and *ex delicto*. The writ system had given way to a law of causes of action. What exactly was a cause of action? According to one judge it was 'simply a factual situation the existence of which entitles one person to obtain from the court a remedy against another person' (Diplock LJ in *Letang v Cooper* [1965] 1 QB 232, 242–243). This is not particularly helpful as a definition but it does illustrate how such causes are dependent upon the categorisation and classification of facts. Thus trespass to land involves a direct invasion of the property while private nuisance involves an indirect invasion; negligence requires the proof of carelessness. These days tort lawyers often talk about rights and duties rather than categories of factual situations, but even at the end of the 20th century one finds an English judge stating that in 'the pragmatic way in which English law has developed, a man's legal rights are in fact those which are protected by a cause of action'. And that it is not in accordance 'with the principles of English law to analyse rights as being something separate from the remedy given to the individual'. So that 'in the ordinary case to establish a legal or equitable right you have to show that all the necessary elements of the cause of action are either present or threatened' (Sir Nicolas Browne-Wilkinson in *Kingdom of Spain v Christie, Manson & Woods Ltd* [1986] 1 WLR 1120, 1129).

As we have seen, many of these causes of action were simply the old personal actions at common law, adorned, to a greater or lesser extent, with some Roman law learning. Thus trespass, detinue, trover (conversion), nuisance, defamation (case) and so on became 'torts' (actions *ex delicto*) while *assumpsit* (damages) and debt came together under a general theory of 'contract' (actions *ex contractu*). Debt also became the basis of actions *quasi ex contractu* (*United Australia Ltd* v *Barclays Bank Ltd* [1941] AC 1, 26–27), now classified, as we have seen, under the independent category of the law of restitution, itself founded on the Roman principle of unjust enrichment (see further Chapter 7).

3.4   COMMON LAW REMEDIES

Yet despite the move to substantive categories (obligations and property), the old actions of trespass and debt remain imprinted on the common law in that damages (trespass and case) and debt remain not just separate remedies but also separate causes of action (*Overstone Ltd* v *Shipway* [1962] 1 WLR 117). In other words, despite the abolition of the forms of action, they continue to be identifiable and independent legal institutions capable of attracting their own rules. In addition to these two monetary remedies, the old action for ejectment has survived as a means of gaining repossession of land (*Manchester Airport Plc* v *Dutton* [2000] 1 QB 133). With respect to moveable property, statute has provided the courts with a kind of *actio in rem* (Torts (Interference with Goods) Act 1977, s 3), although in substance it forms part of the law of tort (that is to say law of obligations). Thus while one mostly studies law from the starting point of substantive categories such as contract, tort, land law and the like (see 5.9 and Chapters 6–7), actual remedies continue to act as focal points for legal rules.

Accordingly an action for *debt* remains a claim for a specific sum of money due either under a contract or as a result of some other legal obligation. 'The plaintiff who claims payment of a debt', said Millett LJ, 'need not prove anything beyond the occurrence of the event or condition on the occurrence of which the debt became due'. And so rules as to remoteness of damage and mitigation of loss are irrelevant (*Jervis* v *Harris* [1996] Ch 195, 202–203). It is, of course, a form of 'specific performance' of a contract since a promise to pay a price for goods sold or services rendered is a primary obligation; the common law court is forcing the contractor to do what he promised to do (*Attica Sea Carriers Corporation* v *Ferrostaal* [1976] 1 Lloyd's Rep 250). *Damages*, the other main common law remedy, 'have been defined as "the pecuniary compensation, obtainable by success in an action, for a wrong which is either a tort or a breach of contract"' and they 'must normally be expressed in a single sum to take account of all the factors applicable to each cause of action' (Lord Hailsham in *Cassell & Co v Broome* [1972] AC 1027, 1070). The rules attaching to damages are of great importance and some, like mitigation, genuinely attach to the remedy of damages itself rather than to the law of contract or tort. One might add that damages at common law are awarded as one lump sum as compensation for damage or loss; however, thanks to statute, they may now be awarded as periodical payments in personal injury cases (Damages Act 1996).

The common law has one (non-statutory) non-monetary remedy, that of *ejectment*. This old personal action has survived as a remedy for the recovery of possession of land by a dispossessed occupier and thus an owner of land 'is entitled to go to the court and obtain an order that the owner "do recover" the land, and to issue a writ of possession immediately' (Lord Denning MR in *McPhail v Persons Unknown* [1973] Ch 447, 457). Until quite recently it was thought that the only persons entitled to ejectment were those who had a right to exclusive occupation of the land and this did not include a person who had a mere contractual right to enter property. However Laws LJ (supported by Kennedy LJ) has asserted that the 'proposition that a plaintiff not in occupation may only obtain the remedy if he is an estate owner assumes that he must bring himself within the old law of ejectment'. This is 'a false assumption' (*Manchester Airport Plc v Dutton* [2000] QB 133, 149). There are today a range of other non-monetary remedies that have been introduced, often as orders, by statute and so, for example, a court can now order repossession of moveable property thanks to the Torts (Interference with Goods) Act 1977.

3.5   EQUITABLE REMEDIES: GENERAL REMARKS

In addition to the common law remedies, the Court of Chancery developed, from the 15th century, a series of remedies to complement the actions of damages and debt. These equitable remedies remain distinct and often attract their own procedural, if not substantive, principles.

The separation between law and equity is one of the distinctive features of the common law tradition even if it now has much less meaning outside of English law. From the historical perspective, the situation in England in the latter part of the 19th century is well summarised in the *First Report of the Judicature Commission 1869* which sets out how the distinction between law and equity 'led to the establishment of two systems of judicature, organized in different ways, and administering justice on different and sometimes opposite principles, using different methods of procedure, and applying different remedies'. The report pointed out that large classes of rights, altogether ignored by the courts of common law, were protected and enforced by the Court of Chancery, and recourse was had to the same court for the purpose of obtaining a more adequate protection against the violation of common law rights than the common law courts were competent to afford. These common law courts were confined by 'their system of procedure in most actions – not brought for recovering the possession of land – to giving judgment for debt and damages, a remedy which has been found to be totally insufficient for the adjustment of the complicated disputes of modern society'. As a result of this report law and equity were merged (Supreme Court of Judicature Act 1875, s 25), but, as it subsequently transpired, only at the level of procedure. Equitable remedies remained independent and they can still exert their own separate influence within contract, tort and restitution (see Chapter 7).

Are there certain general ideas that motivate equitable intervention? One writer has suggested that there were traditionally two broad grounds for intervention by the Court of Chancery, namely abuse of rights and abuse of powers (Weir, 1971, paras 93–102). Now English law does not recognise the civilian notion of an abuse of a right and thus there are a range of situations where equity did not intervene despite the common law seemingly displaying indifference to what some might call abusive behaviour (see *Bradford Corporation v Pickles* [1895] AC 587). It will not, for example, intervene where one contracting party remains silent except in very specific cases where there is a special equitable obligation to inform. Equally it never really interested itself in abusive exclusion clauses in contract, although from an early date it would never enforce penalty clauses. However, where a contractual party insists on enforcing a written term in a contractual document which clearly does not record what was orally agreed between the parties, then the remedy of rectification might well be available. As for abuse of power, equity was and is prepared to restrain owners at common law from using this power in certain ways. Thus a person who transferred property to another on the basis that this other would hold it for the benefit of a third party had only a personal action in contract against the transferee if the latter violated the obligation. Equity took a different view and allowed the beneficiary not only to bring an action against the transferee but, if the transferee had disposed of the property, to follow the property into the hands of others, except a bona fide purchaser for value. Equity will not allow a person who has power over another to abuse this position, for example by convincing the latter to transfer property or property rights to the former (see *Credit Lyonnais Bank Nederland v Burch* [1997] 1 All ER 144).

More specifically equity saw, and sees, itself as being motivated by a range of what are called equitable maxims. Tony Weir extracted the following: 'equity will not suffer a wrong to be without a remedy; equity follows the law; where there is equal equity, the law shall prevail; he who seeks equity must do equity; he who comes into equity must come with clean hands; delay defeats equities; equality is equity; equity looks to the intent rather than to the form; equity looks on that as done which ought to be done; equity imputes an intention to fulfil an obligation; equity acts *in personam*' (Weir, 1971, para 92). As Weir goes on to say, these maxims are far too general to be able to show the more precise effects of equity; yet there are cases where these maxims can be found to have normative force. For example, a debtor who used economic duress to force a creditor to renegotiate the amount of the debt was unable to obtain equitable relief when the creditor decided that he wanted to enforce the original debt (*D & C Builders Ltd v Rees* [1966] 2 QB 617). She did not come to equity with clean hands. In another case delay was fatal in a claim for equitable rescission of a contract (*Leaf v International Galleries* [1950] 2 KB 86).

Two other principles that motivate equity are unjust enrichment and the protection of property. The remedy of specific performance, for example, may be refused if it will result in the claimant being able to extract more money from the defendant contracting party than the claimant would obtain by way of damages at common law (*Co-operative Insurance Society Ltd v Argyll Stores Ltd* [1998] AC 1). And the equitable remedy of account of profits may well be available to relieve a defendant of a profit obtained by dubious means (*English v Dedham Vale Properties Ltd* [1978] 1 WLR 93). As for property, equity has developed a whole structure of trust rights and duties and its remedies have also been used to protect intellectual property interests. However, what is particularly noteworthy is that equity takes a wide view of the notion of property. It will protect confidential information and even once decided that a live performance by the Rolling Stones was a form of property that could be protected by an injunction (*Ex parte Island Records* [1978] Ch 122). This decision was subsequently criticised by the House of Lords (and is now covered by legislation), yet it does illustrate the flexibility of equity's thinking when it comes to defining 'property'. With regard to the law of contract, equity has intervened to prevent a form of justified enrichment becoming an unjustified form (see *Redgrave v Hurd* (1881) 20 Ch D 1) and it sometimes combines this principle with that of protecting property interests (*Beswick v Beswick* [1966] Ch 538 (CA); [1968] AC 58). However equity's attempt to set aside contracts for mistake has been halted by the common law (*The Great Peace* [2003] QB 679). Equity's principles can sometimes find themselves in conflict with the requirement of certainty in commercial law.

3.6   NON-MONETARY EQUITABLE REMEDIES

Given the existence of debt and damages at common law, the majority of the remedies developed in Chancery were non-pecuniary and the principal ones are the following (arranged in importance).

An *injunction* was and remains Chancery's most important remedy and in its paradigm form is a negative order; that is to say it is an order not to do something which acts *in personam* against a defendant. It is, like all equitable remedies, said to be discretionary, although this is not to be taken to mean that judges have complete discretion, for the exercise is governed by equitable principles and of course all decisions have to be motivated. There are particular kinds of injunction including a *mandatory injunction* which is a positive order requiring the defendant to do something (see *Kelsen v Imperial Tobacco Co* [1957] 2 QB 334) and an *interlocutory injunction* (emergency injunction) which is a special emergency form of injunction where the 'object . . . is to protect the plaintiff against injury by violation of his right for which he could not be adequately compensated in damages recoverable in the action if the uncertainty was resolved in his favour at the trial' (*American Cyanamid v Ethicon* [1975] AC 396, 406). In the latter half of the 20th century two particular forms of this remedy were developed. A *Mareva injunction* (freezing order) is one granted to restrain a defendant facing litigation from removing his assets so as to frustrate the claimant (*Mareva Compania Naviera v International Bulk Carriers* [1980] 1 All ER 213). What is important with respect to this injunction is that, although it operates in theory *in personam*, the reality is that its effects are *in rem* (*Allen v Jambo Holdings* [1980] 2 All ER 502). Despite attracting debate, the existence of this particular remedy has been confirmed by statute (Senior Courts Act 1981, s 37(3)) and is now the subject of considerable case-law. An *Anton Piller* (search) order, again supposedly acting only *in personam* against the occupier of premises, is really nothing less than a civil search warrant (*Anton Piller KG v Manufacturing Processes Ltd* [1976] Ch 55); it was developed to combat intellectual property abuses and it is usually applied for *ex parte*, that is to say in secrecy and without the defendant being present in court (*Columbia Picture Inc v Robinson* [1987] Ch 38).

An order for *specific performance* is another type of mandatory order that the Lord Chancellor could make with respect to the enforcement of contracts. However, he would only do this in situations where damages at common law were inadequate and this is the reason why equitable specific performance is often described as an exceptional contract remedy. It is not available 'as of right', although in the case of the sale of land there is a presumption that such a contract will be specifically enforced because land is a unique item and, anyway, the purchaser becomes an equitable owner once contracts are exchanged. As we have seen, equity looks on that as done which ought to be done and so it will force the seller to make the purchaser owner. There are a number of principles that attach to specific performance; for example equity will not enforce a contract if it would require constant supervision by the court (see, for example, *Co-operative Insurance Society Ltd v Argyll Stores Ltd* [1998] AC 1), or if the contract lacks mutuality of obligation (*Price v Strange* [1978] Ch 337), or again if it is a contract for personal services. It may well refuse the remedy if it would cause serious economic inefficiency (*Co-operative Insurance*, above).

In addition to these two leading non-monetary equitable remedies, there are several others. The remedy of *rescission* was developed by the Chancellor in order to set aside contracts if the defendant was guilty of certain kinds of unconscionable behaviour such as misrepresentation, fraud or duress (including undue influence: for a good example see *Credit Lyonnais Bank Nederland v Burch* [1997] 1 All ER 144). It was for a while thought that rescission would be available in certain circumstances for contractual mistake, but this has now been denied by the Court of Appeal (*The Great Peace* [2003] QB 679). Another contractual remedy issuing out of the Court of Chancery that remains of importance in the law of contract is rectification of a contractual (or other) document. Rectification will be ordered if the document clearly does not reflect what was agreed between the parties (*Thomas Bates & Son v Wyndham's (Lingerie) Ltd* [1981] 1 WLR 505). Being an equitable remedy, rectification allows a court to go beyond the text of a written contract (prohibited at common law) and to examine the pre-contractual negotiations (*Daventry DC v Daventry & District Housing Ltd* [2012] 1 WLR 1333). Rectification problems (in equity) may well now find themselves intermixed with contractual interpretation issues (common law) leading to something of a conflict between the two systems.

In the area of restitution, *subrogation* is available where one person 'stands in the shoes' of another person and takes over certain rights of the latter. It has been described as a genuine remedy rather than a cause of action with the result that it can be used in a variety of situations to protect property rights or to prevent unjustified enrichment (*Boscawen v Bajwa* [1995] 4 All ER 769). It is of particular importance in insurance and the law of obligations in that once an insurance company has paid out on a policy it is entitled to be subrogated to any rights the insured might have against third parties responsible for the event that triggered the insurance claim. Such a right does not always work efficiently in that it can be a means of transferring losses from an insurance company (paid to take the risk) to a person who is uninsured (see 7.5).

Another important claim is *tracing*, which in its origin was a remedy in which Chancery recognised that a person could have a right *in rem* in money (or other property) in another person's patrimony (something which is not possible in civilian thinking since money is a consumable item). Whether tracing is an actual remedy is now in question since it has been described as a 'process' rather than a 'remedy' (*Boscawen v Bajwa* [1995] 4 All ER 769), but it certainly was once seen as a kind of *actio in rem*. It remains a proprietary remedy for reclaiming money in another's bank account, although it is normally available only where there is a special equitable 'fiduciary relationship' between the parties (see *Agip (Africa) Ltd v Jackson* [1990] Ch 265 (ChD); [1991] Ch 547 (CA)). In civilian thinking, once money has been transferred title normally passes with the transfer because money is a consumable item. Allowing a person to claim money in another's bank account on the basis of 'ownership' is, then, a genuine Chancery innovation. One might add that it is questionable whether this remedy or process is a non-monetary claim since the end result is the retransfer of the money from defendant to claimant. It might be better therefore to see tracing as a non-monetary process supporting the equitable monetary remedy of account.

In addition to these purely equitable remedies, there are a number of well-established procedural remedies whose equitable origin has now largely disappeared behind civil procedural rules. *Declaration* is where a court is asked merely to declare the rights of the parties and is now a remedy well established in the rules of procedure (see *In re S* [1995] 3 WLR 78). However it originated in the Court of Chancery. Similarly, *discovery of documents* (disclosure) is one of the common law tradition's most famous pretrial remedies (although it is to be found in Roman law: see Dig 2.13), yet it originated in the Chancellor's power to make *in personam* orders against a litigant. The remedy is normally associated with a substantive claim for damages or whatever and is a pretrial procedural order to produce all documents relevant to the substantive claim (see now CPR part 31). But it has also become an independent remedy and can be used, for example, to order a journalist to produce his sources (*X Ltd v Morgan-Grampian (Publishers) Ltd* [1991] 1 AC 1).

Finally, a person with an interest in property which was endangered by the defendant's business behaviour could apply to Chancery for the appointment of a *Receiver* to manage the affairs of the defendant. This is an important remedy in bankruptcy law. This equitable nature of bankruptcy law is equally to be found in the idea that a bankrupt's assets now become the property of a trustee in bankruptcy.

3.7   MONETARY REMEDIES IN EQUITY

As we have seen, monetary remedies are normally associated with the common law courts, but they do have an importance on occasions in equity. An action for an *account of profits* was originally a common law personal action but its procedural nature made it an ideal process for Chancery jurisdiction. The remedy has recently undergone a renaissance in that it is now available as a restitution claim against a defendant who has obtained an unconscionable profit in situations where the claimant has suffered no corresponding provable loss (*Att-Gen v Blake* [2001] 1 AC 268). It is a matter of debate whether or not Chancery could award damages (rather than account). However, thanks to statute, damages can now be awarded in lieu of an injunction or specific performance (Chancery Amendment Act 1858, s 2; now Senior Courts Act 1981, s 50). Damages can also be awarded in lieu of rescission for non-fraudulent misrepresentation (Misrepresentation Act 1967, s 2(2)).

3.8   STATUTORY REMEDIES

In addition to these remedies essentially developed historically by the courts, statute has introduced many remedies of its own (see 7.6). Sometimes legislation makes use of existing remedies such as injunction, damages or even tracing (see for example Proceeds of Crime Act 2002, s 305); sometimes it introduces its own remedy of statutory orders, powers of cancellation or variation or whatever. In particular such statutory orders are to be found in family law legislation and in the Acts regulating the financial, employment and consumer sectors of the economy. Equally statute might take an existing remedy such as damages and extend it to certain heads of damage or interests which might not normally be protected in the ordinary law of contract and tort (see Disability Discrimination Act 1995, s 28V(2); Equality Act 2006, s 68(4)). Often when statute introduces a new cause of action it will lay down provisions as to the remedies available and what interests are protected by these remedies deemed (see Protection from Harassment Act 1997), but it may also deny a particular remedy by establishing certain defences. One notable statutory remedy introduced by the Human Rights Act 1998 (s 8) is that of damages against a public authority that has invaded the human right of the claimant; another notable statutory provision is the granting of a power to use the self-help remedy of reasonable force in certain situations (see, for example, Education and Inspections Act 2006, s 93).

3.9   PUBLIC LAW REMEDIES

The history of the forms of action have, so far, focused almost entirely upon what a civil lawyer would see as 'private law'. Of course some of the writs such as trespass had a public law dimension as well; indeed in one sense the whole common law system was a public rather than a private law procedure in that it was originally an exceptional jurisdiction aimed at protecting the royal interest. Yet there were some writs, mainly associated with the Court of King's Bench, which had a definite public flavour in that they were designed to bring under the control of the common law judges institutions and persons who exercised power through their acts or omissions (see Laws LJ in *R (Cart) v Upper Tribunal* [2010] 2 WLR 1012, paras 44–68).

   However, it has to be stressed at the outset that the history of the common law does not really lend itself to a template that distinguishes between *ius publicum* and *ius privatum*. It is much more helpful to talk in terms of a history of procedure and remedies but then to say that there are important constitutional and administrative dimensions even if they cannot always be clearly separated from private law and the administration of justice. Indeed, this history was to result in a constitutional theory (Dicey) whereby the French dichotomy between *droit public* and *droit privé* was specifically rejected. One might add that the political context of feudalism, within which the early common law developed, was not a model that encouraged a distinction between *imperium* and *dominium* and as a result it is not surprising if the modern law of remedies conforms to a public/private dichotomy only with difficulty (but compare with Boyron, 2010). Accordingly, when one turns to constitutional theory itself, the historical substance is in many ways a history of the powers of the *Curia Regis* and, after its fragmentation, of the royal judges and of Parliament. The history of the common law, in other words, is also a history of constitutional law. Yet of course this is not the whole story. The power struggle between the royal judges and the monarch, and later between judges and Parliament, resulted in legislative texts that can be clearly seen as constitutional documents.

3.10   PREROGATIVE WRITS

From a remedies point of view, the starting point of a history of public law is a group of actions known as the 'prerogative writs'. The origin of these actions is to be found in the royal power of the *Curia Regis* to control all lesser authorities exercising power in the name of the king. This power passed to the judges of the King's Bench and this court assumed a jurisdiction to assure that any judicial or administrative decision should conform to the common law. This jurisdiction was exercised via the prerogative writs, which were originally ordinary procedural processes but which, in the 16th–17th centuries, became a means of judicial control of administrative power (*R (Cart) v Upper Tribunal* [2010] 2 WLR 1012, paras 44–50). As with the 'private' law personal actions at common law, the prerogative writs can be presented simply in terms of a list.

The Writ of *Habeas Corpus* started life as a means of insuring that a defendant appeared in court, but from the 16th century it evolved into a remedy which did almost the opposite. The writ was used to determine if an imprisonment of a subject was valid in law. Thus it became the means of giving expression to the liberty of the subject, a right which itself had been expressed in Magna Carta 1215. In the 18th–19th centuries the scope of the writ had extended beyond imprisonment by a public official or body to, for example, the incarceration of wives by husbands and to questions about the custody of children (family law). Habeas corpus remains an independent remedy today but its scope has been drastically reduced by a whole range of statutes that give powers to the police and sometimes other bodies to detain individuals without trial. It was once a powerful remedy but has been largely neutered by the legislator.

The *Writ of Prohibition* was the oldest of the prerogative writs and was originally used to prevent ecclesiastical courts from hearing cases involving temporal matters. Later it was employed by King's Bench against any inferior court or tribunal that was considered to have been acting beyond its jurisdiction. In the 19th century it was extended even further; it lay against statutory bodies and government departments and thus became a means of controlling administrative, as well as judicial, decisions.

Two writs of particular importance were *mandamus* and *certiorari*. The word *mandamus* means 'we command' and the writ carrying this name was used to restore public offices to those deprived of them. In the 17th century it developed into a means of controlling local authorities: the writ commanded the authority to act or to show cause why it did not. In the 19th and 20th century the writ was used to compel public bodies to exercise their statutory duties. The writ of *certiorari* was originally used to remove a case from an inferior court to King's Bench and thus acted as a means not just of assuming jurisdiction but also of reviewing cases (although only criminal). It was later extended to administrative bodies and thus *certiorari* became a general procedure for reviewing criminal cases from inferior courts and orders issued by public officials or bodies. It could not be used as a method of appeal as such since the review applied only to an examination of the record to ensure that an order or conviction was not *ultra vires*. But in the 20th century the huge growth in administrative tribunals resulted in a renewed life for *certiorari*; it became the procedural means for Queen's Bench to examine the decisions of administrative bodies and to correct errors in law. If such errors were found the decision of the public body could be quashed. In other words it was a remedy by which the judges of the common law could review, and quash if necessary, the judicial (as opposed to administrative) decisions of public bodies and public officials.

These writs survived the abolition of the forms of action in 1852 and 1875, but, with the exception of habeas corpus, became 'orders' in 1938 (Administration of Justice (Miscellaneous Provisions) Act 1938, s 7). In 1977 these orders were combined to form a single action of *judicial review* and this term is gradually eclipsing the old labels such as *mandamus* and *certiorari* (Senior Courts Act 1981, s 31), although habeas corpus has survived as an independent writ as a result of its constitutional and ideological importance (http://www.adminlaw.org.uk/docs/habeas-corpus.htm). Procedure is now governed by Part 54 of the CPR 1998. Interestingly case-law has suggested there is a difference between public and private law that applies to the distinction between judicial review on the one hand and the other ordinary remedies such as debt and damages on the other (*O'Reilly v Mackman* [1983] 2 AC 237), but this has been rejected by doctrine as being historically and conceptually inaccurate (see Oliver, 2001). Many of the principles of administrative law have actually been taken from areas of private law such as trusts and company law.

3.11   EQUITABLE REMEDIES AND PUBLIC LAW

In addition to these prerogative writs, the Court of Chancery developed a series of non-monetary remedies, two of which became particularly important in the area of 'public law'. The Court of Chancery seemingly always had an inherent power to issue a declaratory judgment, that is to say a judgment that simply declared a right but did not follow it with any specific relief (*Guaranty Trust Co of New York v Hannay & Co* [1915] 2 KB 536, 568). However, because of the reluctance of English judges to issue advisory opinions, this remedy did not become important until the 19th century and after. Nevertheless in the field of public law the declaration was of particular importance with respect to disputes against the Crown because the judges felt that they could not issue coercive remedies against their own 'employer' so to speak. Declarations were different. And indeed it seems that this remedy may have been used by the common law courts, as well as Chancery, perhaps as early as the 16th century (Lawson, 1980,

234). Whatever the historical situation, the declaration became a general public law remedy in the 20th century thanks to the Crown Proceedings Act 1947 (s 21). Declaration, it should be noted, is wider than *certiorari* (see *Pyx Granite Co v Ministry of Housing* [1958] 1 All ER 625, 632). One might also note that the remedy adopted by the Human Rights Act 1998 (s 4) in respect of legislation that contravenes the European Convention is declaration and not a power to anul the offending text.

The second Chancery remedy is of course the *injunction*. This remedy, because of its flexibility, 'made it a weapon particularly suitable for checking the action of public authorities encroaching on property rights'. Indeed,

> it is not at all surprising that the principles on which judicial control was exercised, namely, the so-called rules of *natural justice* and the doctrine of *ultra vires*, were first expressed and expounded in cases relating to an action for injunction as well as, or even earlier than, in cases concerning prerogative writs (Galeotti, 1954, 31).

In the 19th century the injunction, along with declaration, became an important public, as well as private, law remedy. However, from the 18th century, an individual could not claim an injunction against a public body unless some 'private' interest of his was in issue (private right or special damage); the individual had to claim the remedy via the Attorney General in a relator action (see generally *Gouriet v Union of Post Office Workers* [1978] AC 435). Today an injunction against a public body is claimed by way of judicial review proceedings if the matter in issue is one of public law.

3.12   JUDICIAL REVIEW

The prerogative writs, with the exception of habeas corpus, have been abolished in form but remain – along with the two equitable remedies (declaration and injunction) – as remedies available in an action for judicial review. The grounds for obtaining such a review were summed up by Lord Diplock: the 'first ground [is] "illegality", the second "irrationality" and the third "procedural impropriety"' (*Council of Civil Service Unions v Minister for the Civil Service* [1985] AC 374, 410). These grounds should not be seen as watertight compartments since administrative law is always developing; but they do help one to distinguish between an action for judicial review and an appeal against a decision of a court or tribunal. An action for judicial review does not concern itself with the substance of a decision but only with its legality. It is not for the judges to judge the fairness of the administrative decision under review and so they cannot substitute their decision in place of the decision taken by a public official; all they can do is to quash the decision. In contrast when appeal judges allow an appeal they substitute their decision for that of the court below. Nevertheless the two procedures do share something of a common history and, of course, the continental review of a judgment by a *Cour de cassation* seems closer to a judicial review process than to an appeal (see 2.8).

Three important requirements for judicial review need to be mentioned. The first is that the person bringing the action must have 'sufficient interest' in the matter (Senior Courts Act 1981, s 31(3)). If, then, a claimant can show no connection with the contested decision then such a person will be barred from bringing the action for lack of *locus standi.* Does an environmental body such as Greenpeace have sufficient interest in a ministerial decision to allow, say, nuclear waste to be discharged into the atmosphere? One can see that such a procedural question has an enormous impact on environmental 'rights' (*R v Inspectorate of Pollution, ex p Greenpeace (No 2)* [1994] 4 All ER 329). In fact one can reverse the situation in order to indicate that a person does not have to have a 'right' before he can claim judicial review. A citizen only has to have an interest or, better, a 'legitimate expectation' and thus it could be said that English law shares with continental law the idea that private law is about protecting rights whereas administrative law is about protecting interests and expectations. A second fundamental requirement is that the defendant is a public body: the remedy of judicial review is not available against private persons or entities. However, the test for public body is not a formal but a functional one and so a private body may be open to an action if it is performing a public function (*R (Beer) v Hampshire Farmers' Markets Ltd* [2004] 1 WLR 233). The third requirement is that judicial review is a remedy of last resort. It should not be permitted 'if a significant part of the issues between the parties could be resolved outside the litigation process' (*R (Cowl) v Plymouth CC (Practice Note)* [2002] 1 WLR 803, para 14).

3.13   DEBT AND DAMAGES CLAIMS IN PUBLIC LAW

A final question that needs to be considered with respect to judicial review is whether or not the action includes a claim for damages. The answer is both yes and no. The actual formal remedy of judicial review does not in itself permit a claim for damages because the old prerogative writs were not damages actions. Accordingly a claimant must prove that he has a cause of action in contract or tort before damages can be awarded. However, a claimant does not need to bring a separate claim and so the judicial review proceedings can be used to claim damages; but, of course, they will only be awarded if they would have been awarded in a separate claim.

The reason for this complexity is to be found in history. All of the old prerogative and Chancery remedies were non-monetary claims and could not be used by a claimant to obtain compensation. If the plaintiff wished to obtain damages, then one of the 'private' law writs had to be used of which the most important was the writ of trespass and its later offshoots based on the Action on the Case. In fact it is misleading to see trespass as a 'private law' remedy since it was equally available against public bodies, except of course the Crown, for there was no court superior to the king and thus he was above the law. Later, this non-liability thesis was replaced by the idea that 'The King can do no wrong'. However, individual public officers could be liable in trespass and so could public bodies that did not fall within the scope of the Crown. A local authority was, for example, held liable in trespass to the owner of a house it demolished without going through the proper legal procedures (*Cooper v Wandsworth Board of Works* (1863) 143 ER 414). This rule about damages has, then, been preserved in respect of an action for judicial review and thus if a claimant wants compensation (in addition to a judicial review order), then liability in contract or tort must be established.

After 1932 negligence became a distinct cause of action thanks to *Donoghue v Stevenson* ([1932] AC 562) and is now the tort that is most commonly used in damages actions against public bodies for harm caused non-intentionally. Much of the case-law is simply integrated into the law of tort and thus forms part of the ordinary law of obligations (see Chapter 7). However, during the last couple of decades actions against public bodies have formed a distinct part of the law of torts in many doctrinal publications and so it is now possible to isolate within the common law a distinct area of 'administrative liability' (see further Samuel, 2008, 329–359). With respect to the Crown, its special status was preserved well into the 20th century, but Crown liability was modified by the Crown Proceedings Act 1947. It has to be stressed that, formally speaking, an action against a public body or the Crown for negligence (or any other tort) is no different from an action against any private body or person. However in substance special policy factors often come into play and these usually are to be found in, for example, the duty of care or causation questions (see generally Samuel, 2010, 210–212). In addition to actions in negligence, a public body can also be liable in other torts such as nuisance and breach of statutory duty. The tort of misfeasance in public office is only available against a public agent or body, but malicious prosecution can be brought against a private individual.

As regards actions for debt, it would seem that the public and private distinction is of marginal importance. Debts can be claimed against public bodies in the same way as they are claimed in private law. One reason for this is that the same law of contract applies equally to public as to private bodies (but see Davies, 2008). In fact even in situations where the debt arises out of a statutory relationship the court will still treat the claim as one involving a private right and the action will be one as if it is a contractual debt (*Roy v Kensington & Chelsea & Westminster Family Practitioner Committee* [1992] 1 AC 624). Actions for damages in contract are treated in much the same way. If a public body is in breach of a contract with a private party the latter can claim damages in the normal way (see, for example, *Blackpool & Fylde Aero Club Ltd v Blackpool BC* [1990] 1 WLR 1195; see 4.9); equally a public body can sue a private person – or indeed another public body – for breach of contract. Indeed there are cases of one public body suing another in tort or contract thus indicating that even public entities have 'private' rights (see, for example, *Ministry of Housing and Local Government v Sharp* [1970] 2 QB 223).

3.14 SELF-HELP REMEDIES

Mention must finally be made of remedies that are available without the aid of the court. These are called self-help remedies of which the most well known is probably the 'right' of self-defence. One can use force to repel a trespass but only if the force used is reasonable in the circumstances. If it is not reasonable, then the person using self-help will himself be liable in trespass (*Revill v Newbery* [1996] QB 567). However, in addition to this self-defence remedy, there are others which are, perhaps, less dramatic but actually of considerable importance. The victim of a breach of contract has, if the breach is fundamental, the right to terminate the contract and if the breach amounts to a complete non-performance the other party may be entitled to refuse to pay the price (*Bolton v Mahadeva* [1972] 1 WLR 1009). As with self-defence, care must be taken because if the breach was not fundamental, the person who terminates the contract will himself be in breach and may be liable in damages for any losses caused by the termination. Set-off is also a self-help remedy. Where two contracting parties owe each other money one party can, if the debts are connected, set off against what he owes to his creditor what this latter owes to him. Thus if D owes C £500 and C owes D £200, D need pay only £300 to C (for a history of set-off see *Eller v Grovecrest Investments Ltd* [1995] QB 272). An unpaid repairer of, for example, a motorcar can use the self-help remedy of keeping possession of the vehicle until the owner pays for the repairs;

this remedy is known as a lien (see *Tappenden v Artus* [1964] 2 QB 185). Another self-help remedy is abatement of a nuisance; a neighbour can, for example, cut off the branches of a tree that encroaches onto his property and is a nuisance.

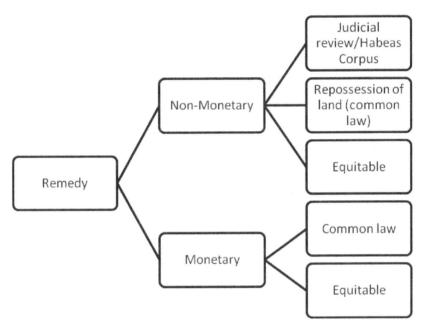

Figure 3.1   General types of remedy in English law

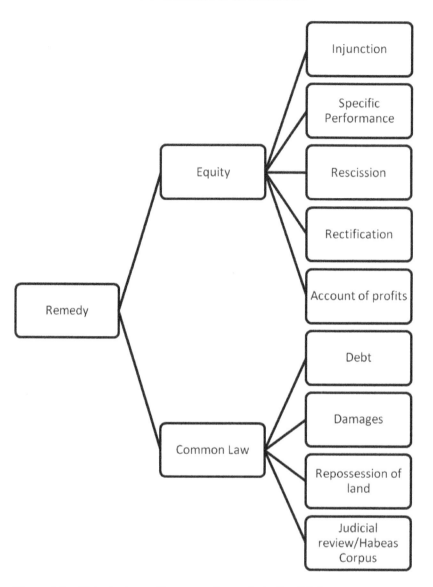

Figure 3.2   Principal specific types of remedy in English law

4. English legal education and English legal thought (1): sources and methods

What, then, is the conceptual structure and foundation of the common law? This is by no means an easy question because much will depend upon the ontological and epistemological (philosophy of knowledge) focal points chosen. If one sees all legal systems as models of rules, then learning the common law will consist of learning its rules and how these rules fit together as a whole. If some other focal point is chosen, then a different model will emerge.

With respect to the civil law the history and the transmission of a certain type of legal knowledge via Justinian's *Institutes* and *Digest* have largely determined the epistemological and ontological foundation. However the history of the common law proves much more ambiguous and allows for a number of rather different models. Is it a system of categories and rules? Is it a system of rights and duties? Or is it, as some have often implied, just a collection of institutions and remedies? Certainly studying the courts and the procedures is not enough to gain a full knowledge of the English (or common law) mentality. Accordingly in this chapter and those that follow the focus shifts from judicial institutions to legal education and to legal method and thought in general.

Once again the contrasts with the civil law tradition are striking. In the civilian world university law professors have been central in shaping the whole tradition itself. In the English common law world professors have, until relatively recently, been at best marginal. However, just because the common law has been formed and shaped by judges and practitioners, this does not mean that legal institutions and concepts are not of central importance. They are, even if they turn out to be different from those in the civil law.

4.1 LEARNING THE COMMON LAW: HISTORICAL CONSIDERATIONS

The historical emphasis so far has been on what might be termed the practical institutions of the common law: that is to say on the courts, the jury, the procedures and remedies. In many ways this emphasis stands in sharp contrast to the history of the civil law where the primary institution was the university and its corps of law professors. The history of the civil law is largely (but not exclusively) a history of the teaching of Roman law (see Stein, 1999). In England and Wales there were no such teaching institutions before the 19th century and legal education was thus for many centuries in the hands of practitioners, that is to say the Inns of Court, which were professional organisations not dissimilar to Oxford or Cambridge colleges.

The Inns began their life as lodgings for the advocates (serjeants-at-law, later in the 15th century called barristers) who controlled and presented cases to the Court of Common Pleas, but they developed into colleges that provided lectures, moots and general discussion. Thus in the early centuries of the common law, it was the Inns that offered a legal education and this was supplemented by attendance in court where judges would, as well as presiding over cases, explain to students what was going on. As for the universities of Oxford and Cambridge, they taught only Roman law, a subject of no interest to those practising the common law; this civilian education was studied mainly by men going into the Church. 'At its height', observes a leading English legal historian, 'the professional law school was tough and effective; but . . . it came to an abrupt end in the middle of the seventeenth century, leaving self-help as the principal method of legal education'. In other words a law student would gather his law 'from such books as he could afford to buy or borrow; and the most useful of these owed more to the alphabet than to schematic analysis' (Baker, 2002, 170). In the middle of the 18th century William Blackstone began to give lectures on the common law at Oxford – lectures that were to become the *Commentaries on the Laws of England* (1765–1769) and to acquire a status analogous to the *Institutes* in Roman law – but this development, important as it was, did not stimulate a new dawn in English legal education. Lectures on the common law might well have been given at both Oxford and Cambridge from the 17th century but they often suffered from a lack of audience. The same was true of lectures on the common law offered elsewhere in the first half of the 19th century.

4.2   REFORM OF LEGAL EDUCATION

Change came in the second half of the 19th century. A Select Committee on Legal Education, established by the English Parliament, reported in 1846 that 'the present state of legal education in England and Ireland . . . is extremely unsatisfactory and incomplete, and exhibits a striking contrast and inferiority to such education . . . at present in operation in all the more civilised states of Europe and America'. Indeed the report concluded that no legal education worthy of the name was to be found in England and Ireland. As the report noted, this stood in stark contrast to the situation in continental Europe where there has been a tradition of legal education from Roman to modern times.

The report of 1846 was to stimulate a change of attitude with regard to the teaching of law in England (Scotland was quite different) with the result that, today, there are well over 70 law schools in England and Wales. The change of attitude was not confined just to institutional development; the universities – at that time primarily Oxford and Cambridge – and the Inns of Court 'took steps to provide a legal education of the scientific character required by the Report' (Stein, 1980, 79). And this scientific character meant, in effect, the study of Roman law since English law, however strong it might have been in terms of its detailed rules and remedies, was weak on legal theory. As Stein notes, while 'English law has remained relatively free of Roman influences, English jurisprudence [legal theory and legal philosophy] has traditionally turned for inspiration to the current continental theories, necessarily based on Roman law' (Stein, 1980, 123). At the level of legal education, then, there was from the 19th century until right into the 20th century an almost harmonised vision in Europe of legal science founded on a set of universal concepts fashioned in particular by the German civil lawyers of this period. This harmony at the level of theory was, in the longer term, to be ruptured by a movement in USA known as American Realism.

4.3   MODERN LEGAL EDUCATION

The 1846 report, as we have seen, encouraged the development of a corps of law professors, but as Richard Card has noted, the 'growth of university legal education was a slow business'. By 'the end of the nineteenth century . . . it could fairly be said that that the academic study of law was firmly established, but even then there were only ten law schools in England and Wales' and the 'number had only increased to 29 by the early 1970s'. Moreover until 'the early 1950s they relied to a great extent on staff who were in full-time legal practice' and it was only 'from the 1950s that university law schools began the transition to their present character' (SPTL Presidential Address, 2002). High-quality and research-orientated legal education is, in short, a very modern phenomenon as far as the English common law is concerned and this in turn accounts for the lack of what a civil lawyer would see as scientific works. The common law had no Cujas or Donellus and its first 'Domat' or 'Pothier' was Blackstone, whose success was assured by applying the Roman institutional scheme to the English legal material (Cairns, 1984).

One result of this absence of a long historical tradition of professorial doctrine was that when a class of university jurists began to emerge during the 20th century they were treated for much of the century with a certain indifference, if not disdain, by practitioners and judges. Academic doctrine was cited in judgments only when the authors were dead, and both the Bar and the Law Society once regarded – indeed some members still regard – the university law school as 'a complete waste of time', these professionals preferring 'people who have read some other subject at university' (see Birks, 1998, 404). Things are to an extent changing: more enlightened senior judges, some with law degrees and even faculty teaching experience, decreed at the end of the 20th century that doctrine as well as cases and statutes should now be presented in argument and the value of comparative law is equally making itself felt (see, for example, *Fairchild v Glenhaven Funeral Services Ltd* [2003] 1 AC 32). However, the long years of disdain had the effect of edging a section of legal scholarship away from analysis and commentary on the common law itself and into high-level legal theory and beyond; a section of doctrine, in other words, has become divorced from the positive law as found in the cases and statutes.

This divorce has been encouraged by the statistical fact that only around half of English law graduates enter the legal profession. A percentage of academic lawyers accordingly see themselves as social scientists as much as jurists, their primary duty being one geared towards providing a liberal university education rather than professional training (Cownie, 2004). Other academic lawyers, who see the university degree as a vital part of a technical legal education, regret this situation; it is a retreat into the 'ivory tower' and perhaps ultimately destructive of law itself (see, for example, Birks, 1998). Whatever one's views, the divorce has not been without its intellectual effects, the principal one being that what constitutes legal 'knowledge' is arguably much wider in Anglo-American law faculties than in French ones (Jestaz & Jamin, 2004, 264–301). Many different currents of thought have developed – feminist jurisprudence, critical legal studies, law and literature to name just some (Jestaz & Jamin, 2004, 287–296)

– and this has in its turn stimulated thinking and debate in common law faculties. It has to be said that the centre of such innovative thinking has not actually been the United Kingdom but the United States where the relationship between law schools and the legal profession is not quite the same. Nevertheless, many in the American legal profession have noted an increasing gulf between the law schools and practice. One might perhaps draw an historical analogy between the *mos Gallicus* and the *mos Italicus*, the former also being considered in its time as professorial and of little use to practitioners (Jones, 1940, 42).

4.4   IMPACT OF AMERICAN REALISM

Some see this American legal culture as having its origin in a long-term struggle against formalism and in the attempt to profit from advances made in disciplines other than law. Of these movements the one that was to prove decisive in terms of a comparative analysis of legal knowledge in the civilian and the common law traditions is arguably American Realism (Jestaz & Jamin, 2004, 273–284). This movement, as diverse as it was – Twining calls it 'an historical phenomenon' – can essentially be summed up by reference to the title of an article by Felix Cohen (1907–1953), namely 'Transcendental Nonsense and the Functional Approach' (Cohen, 1935). Law and legal knowledge were to be defined and understood not as a set of abstract norms and systematised concepts, but strictly in terms of their function. This shift of scheme of intelligibility generated a mass of academic literature that put the emphasis on legal cases and how they are decided, such doctrine asserting that legal decisions are not the result of the application of an abstract rule applied to an objective set of facts via the syllogism. Instead the solutions of cases result from social and psychological factors such as the educational and cultural background of the judge and the way facts are constructed (never objective). This movement was denounced as dangerous and nihilistic, but its longer-term impact on the teaching of law in the common law world was, as Twining points out, that there is more to the study of law than the study of a system of rules. Most Anglo-American teachers – and indeed a good many practitioners – would, like Twining, regard this as a truism, thus giving substance to his observation that 'we are all realists now' (Twining, 1973, 382). The end result is a legal literature in the common law world that is much more diversified than *la doctrine* in France (Jestaz & Jamin, 2004, 267).

4.5 SPIRIT OF NON-CODIFICATION

Nevertheless, one should not allow the impact of American Realism to eclipse other aspects of English doctrine. As we have seen, one effect of the 1846 report was to encourage the teaching of legal science and this proved important when the forms of action were abolished in 1852. The latter half of the 19th century is marked by frequent references in judgments to Roman, French and German texts and, indeed, the fashioning of a general theory of contract by the judges during this century can be regarded as something of a 'reception' of civil law, although English contract law does display a distinctive character when compared with civilian contractual thinking (see Samuel, 2007a and 7.2–3). The fact was that the abolition of the forms of action had left a vacuum and this was filled at first by continental ideas and categories, which at that time had the status of science.

This input of civilian legal science had quite profound effects on English doctrine, some of which were to last well into the 20th century. For example, Kevin and Susan Gray (2003) show how writers on land law attempted to raise their subject to the status of an axiomatic science and Steve Hedley (1999) charts the 19th-century codification movement in England which resulted, if not in a general civil code, at least in the codification of sale of goods, partnership and a few other specific areas of commercial law. The point to be stressed is that during the late 19th century and first half of the 20th century English academic writing on law was heavily influenced by civil law methods. Even in the middle of the 20th century the 'good' English law textbook is described as one which is more than just a guide to the case-law: 'they seek not only to arrange the cases systematically but to extract from them the general principles of the law and to show how those principles may be developed' (Jolowicz, 1963, 314–315). The role of the academic, in other words, is to use the methods of science – induction and deduction – so as to produce a legal knowledge that is validated by its internal coherence and its tendency towards objective legal certainty.

Yet the codification movement itself failed. The reason, according to Hedley, was that the growth of university law faculties, instead of encouraging codification, actually stymied the possibility by doctrinally representing the common law as a coherent system of rules. One might add that even if a civil code had been promulgated the movement would still, over the longer term, have probably failed, as evidence from the USA (and indeed from the English Sale of Goods Act 1893) suggests. The *mentalité* of the common law judge, and of the 20th-century legislator, would have conspired to transform the code, through interpretation and legislative amendment, into just another dense area of law in which the facts of cases, rather than the purity of the original text, would be at the basis of legal knowledge. The alphabet would over time have come to subvert any axiomatic scheme. For as Gray and Gray conclude (after exhaustive research into land law cases and doctrine), the common law mentality is one where the '*axiomatic* has given way to the *axiological* (in the sense of a pervasive concern with the values which underpin legal phenomena)' and the 'concept of law which emerges from this analysis is one founded upon collaborative social practices of intellectual exchange or dialectic; it is born of a more authentic perception of the common law as a species of customary law' (2003, 230). Professor Waddams (2003) reaches a similar conclusion (on which see Samuel, 2005) and Professor Legrand (1996) argues that all this undermines any idea of a European civil code. As for legal education itself, both Professor Cownie (2004) and Professor McCrudden (2006) suggest that all law teachers see themselves to a greater or lesser extent as 'socio-legal' now.

4.6   PRECEDENT

English law may exhibit a spirit of non-codification but this does not mean that it sees itself as a system without structure and coherence. Structure and stability are said to be provided, instead, by the doctrine of precedent which can be summed up as follows: 'in the hierarchical system of courts which exists in this country, it is necessary for each lower tier, including the Court of Appeal, to accept loyally [as binding] the decisions of the higher tiers' (Lord Hailsham LC in *Broome v Cassell & Co Ltd* [1972] AC 1027, 1054). The necessity for precedent is in turn rooted in the need for certainty (see, for example, Practice Direction [1966] 1 WLR 1234). It has to be said, of course, that the idea of precedent is not something unique to the common law. There is evidence in Roman law that authority attached to lines of decisions by jurists and in modern civil it would be idle to say that great authority does not attach to decisions of supreme courts (Jolowicz, 1963, 220–226). However, there is no theory of precedent as such in the civil law. In the common law there is such a theory, although it is by no means static.

The impression is often given that the doctrine of precedent is something as old as the common law itself. Yet a moment's reflection should indicate that this cannot be the case. Before the 16th century there was little substantive law because the whole trial process was centred on the jury verdict; the judge was little more than a referee and questions of pure law rarely surfaced (see 1.4). And even up to the 19th century there was no proper hierarchical system of courts, decisions of fact (in common law courts) were still decided by a jury who never gave reasons for their verdicts and there were few reliable law reports. It is really only during the 19th century, especially with the establishment of official law reports in 1866 and the reorganisation of the courts into a proper hierarchy in 1875, that one sees a formalised theory of precedent establishing itself (Jolowicz, 1963, 230). And this theory only lasted just over a century before it began to break down, or at least retreat back into the older idea of a search for principle (Practice Direction [2001] 1 WLR 194). Thus common law judges, in the last few years, have indicated their reservations about precedent even if they refuse to go as far as saying that it is now extinct and should be avoided.

The first major step in this retreat from strict precedent was the Practice Direction ([1966] 1 WLR 1234) issued by the House of Lords indicating that a 'too rigid adherence to precedent may lead to injustice in a particular case and also unduly restrict the proper development of the law'; the Law Lords proposed therefore 'to depart from a previous decision when it appears right to do so'. A second step is Lord Goff's 1983 lecture where he said the 'answer must lie both in not adopting too strict a view of the doctrine of precedent, and yet according sufficient respect to it to enable it to perform its task of ensuring not merely stability in law, but consistency in its administration'. He went on to note that in the past 'there appeared to exist some judges who saw the law almost as a deductive science, a matter of finding the relevant authorities and applying them to the facts of the particular case'. This is, he said, no longer the case; judges cannot disregard or ignore precedents but they see themselves at liberty to adapt or qualify them to ensure a legally just result on the facts before them (Goff, 1983 (1999)). Perhaps, then, 'the enduring strength of the common law is that it has been developed on a case-by-case basis by judges for whom the attainment of practical justice was a major objective of their work' (Lord Steyn in *Att-Gen v Blake* [2001] 1 AC 268, 292).

As for the actual operation of precedent, it is not cases that bind but 'their rationes decidendi do' (*R (Kadhim) v Brent Housing Board* [2001] QB 955, para 16). Yet discovering the *ratio*, as Lord Denning MR once pointed out, can be a difficult task, especially as the *ratio* has to be distinguished from any *obita dicta* (things said by the by the way) which are not binding (*The Hannah Blumenthal* [1983] 1 AC 854, 873–875). What, then, is meant by the expression? The most important point to stress is that the *ratio decidendi* of a case is not an abstract rule or principle to be induced out of a case subsequently to be applied in a deductive fashion as if the rule was a code provision. This is not to say that induction, deduction and the syllogism have no formal (or ideological) role. But the *ratio* 'is almost always to be ascertained by an analysis of the material facts of the case'

(*Lupton v FA & AB Ltd* [1972] AC 634, 658 per Lord Simon). It is this notion of the 'material facts' of a case that holds the key to the application of a precedent in that a comparison must always be made between the facts of the case in hand and the facts of any precedent.

4.7 PRECEDENT AND LEGAL REASONING

This analogy point is worth developing since Lord Simon's analysis of legal method makes a number of important formal methodological points. He states that a

> judicial decision will often be reached by a process of reasoning which can be reduced into a sort of complex syllogism, with the major premise consisting of a pre-existing rule of law (either statutory or judge-made) and with the minor premise consisting of the material facts of the case under immediate consideration.

The conclusion, he says, may or may not establish new law, but where it does 'frequently the new law will appear only from subsequent comparison of, on the one hand, the material facts inherent in the major premise with, on the other, the material facts which constitute the minor premise'. And as 'a result of this comparison it will often be apparent that a rule has been extended by an analogy expressed or implied' (*Lupton, supra*, pp 658–659). Lord Simon explained the method using *Rylands v Fletcher* ((1866) LR 1 Ex 265 (Ex); (1868) LR 3 HL 330 (HL)) as an example. This precedent concerned the escape of water; when a new case came along involving the escape of electricity it was not just a matter of applying a rule about 'anything likely to do mischief if it escapes'. The court had to decide if electricity was analogous to water; if it were not, the precedent would not apply. If it were, then the relevant analogy for the future would be electricity.

One might note two points here. First, this reasoning by analogy is of particular importance when it comes to extending the tort of negligence (duty of care) to new factual situations; the approach is not one of applying an abstract principle like *Code Civil* (CC) art 1382 to a set of facts. The new situation needs to be analogous to the facts of an existing duty of care case (*Caparo Industries plc v Dickman* [1990] 2 AC 605, 635). Secondly, and perhaps unconsciously, Lord Simon himself goes far in undermining the 'syllogism' aspect to common law legal method. The key focal point is whether electricity is analogous to water. And the answer to this question is not to be found using Aristotelian logic. Rather, it is a matter of comparing images (see further Samuel, 2003).

4.8   POLICY REASONING

Reasoning by analogy is not the only technique employed by the judges. 'In previous times', said Lord Denning, 'when faced with a new problem, the judges have not openly asked themselves the question: what is the best policy for the law to adopt?' However, he continued, 'the question has always been there in the background' and has been concealed behind other questions about duty, proximity, foreseeability and so on (*Dutton v Bognor Regis UDC* [1972] 1 QB 373, 397). Despite the criticism this approach has received, it is common for judges even in the House of Lords and now Supreme Court to appeal on occasions to policy. Thus in one 'administrative liability' case Lord Keith asserted, 'in my opinion there is another reason why an action for damages in negligence should not lie against the police in circumstances such as those of the present case, and that is public policy' (*Hill v Chief Constable of West Yorkshire* [1989] AC 53, 63; see also *Elguzouli-Daf v Commissioner of Police of the Metropolis* [1995] QB 335).

Just what is meant by policy is of course an interesting question (Waddams, 2011, 14). One judge has said that it can be seen as a means of identifying 'social interests beyond the purely legal which call for the modification of a normal legal rule' (Lord Simon in *D v NSPCC* [1978] AC 171, 235). And in the Court of Appeal decision of *Barclays Bank v O'Brien* ([1993] QB 109) one of the judges used policy as a means of solving a problem that he felt could not be dealt with by recourse to precedent. The precedents were ambiguous and could be used to justify a decision one way or the other. 'The choice should', said Scott LJ, 'be a matter of policy.' This use of policy would give rise to a social question: 'Ought the law to treat married women who provide security for their husband's debts, and others in an analogous position, as requiring special protection?' (at 139). Here again, of course, one is looking beyond the text to the interests in play. However, this appeal to an interest through the use of policy does not solve the problem of ambiguity; for, in the House of Lords' decision in *O'Brien*, Lord Browne-Wilkinson focused on a quite different interest. In place of the social interest of wives he emphasised the economic interest of business enterprise. 'If the rights secured to wives by the law renders vulnerable loans granted on the security of matrimonial homes', said the Law Lord, 'institutions will be unwilling to accept such security, thereby reducing the flow of loan capital to business enterprises.' It was for him 'essential that a law designed to protect the vulnerable does not render the matrimonial home unacceptable as security to financial institutions' ([1994] 1 AC 180, 188).

Another way of viewing policy is as a matter of social or practical justice. It represents the pragmatic approach of the common law which 'has not always developed on strictly logical lines'. And 'where logic leads down a path that is beset with practical difficulties the courts have not been frightened to turn aside and seek the pragmatic solution that will best serve the needs of society' (Griffiths LJ in *Ex parte King* [1984] 3 All ER 897, 903). This pragmatic approach can now be seen in terms of policy. One judge has said that we now live in 'a less formalist age' and that policy is an issue that arises when more than one 'solution is logically defensible'. In the area of contract 'good sense, fairness and respect for the reasonable expectations of contracting parties suggests that the best solution' is one which 'at least has the merit of promoting more sensible results than any other solution' (Steyn LJ in *Watts v Aldington* (1993) The Times, 16 December 1993 quoted in *Jameson v CEGB* [1997] 3 WLR 151, 161).

This 'sensible solution' approach was particularly evident in Lord Denning's judgment in the *Spartan Steel* case where the issue was whether pure economic loss could be recovered from a defendant who had carelessly cut off the electricity supply to the claimant's factory (*Spartan Steel & Alloys Ltd v Martin & Co* [1973] 1 QB 27). 'At bottom I think the question of recovering economic loss is one of policy', said the then Master of the Rolls (at 36). For one must consider the nature of the hazard. According to Lord Denning, the cutting off of electricity is a hazard that everyone has to face and it usually results in economic loss that is not very large. Most people, he claimed, take the risk of such losses upon themselves and 'they do not go running round to their solicitor'. The policy to be pursued here, accordingly, was one of recognising that this 'is a healthy attitude which the law should encourage' (38).

Yet another way of viewing the policy approach is from the position of social science method: the approach of Lord Denning in *Spartan Steel* can be seen as a form of functionalism. That is to say a rule is judged not by its literal meaning but by its envisaged function. Lord Denning, having examined the pure economic loss rule in negligence in terms of its history in the case-law, abandons precedent as such to justify the application of the rule by reference to the fact that when the supply of electricity is cut off it affects a multitude of persons by putting them to inconvenience and sometimes causing economic loss. However, such 'a hazard is regarded by most people as a thing they must put up with – without seeking compensation from anyone'. In other words, the economic loss rule has as its *function* the aim of discouraging litigation and it is this function that, for Lord Denning, gives the rule its normative force.

This approach of Lord Denning MR in *Spartan Steel* came in for criticism by the then Professor of Legal Philosophy at the University of

Oxford. According to Ronald Dworkin (see 5.4–6), a judicial decision in a hard case like *Spartan Steel* 'should be generated by principle not policy' (Dworkin, 1977, 84). An argument of policy, says Dworkin, is one which justifies the advancement or protection of some collective goal of the community as a whole. For example the argument that a subsidy should be paid to aircraft manufacturers in order to protect the defence of the nation would be an argument of policy. An argument of principle, on the other hand, is one that advances or secures 'some individual or group right' (1977, 82). Now if an aircraft manufacturer sues to recover such a subsidy it would not argue the case on the ground that the national defence would be enhanced by the subsidy; the argument would be based strictly on its right to the subsidy (1977, 83). This, asserts Dworkin, is right and proper since judges are not elected and thus are not responsible to the electorate in the same way as the legislator. It is for the legislator to make policy and to pass laws founded on, inter alia, arguments of policy. As for judges, they 'should be as unoriginal as possible' (1977, 84) because it seems 'wrong to take property from the individual and hand it to another in order just to improve overall economic efficiency' (at 85).

4.9   ANALYSING A CASE

Direct appeals to policy might attract academic criticism, but even when there is no direct appeal the dialectical nature of the oral legal argument in a common law case can often allow functional arguments to trump more formal ones. This is why legal education needs to embrace detailed analysis of individual cases.

Take the following example. In *Blackpool & Fylde Aero Club Ltd v Blackpool BC* ([1990] 1 WLR 1195) a local authority invited tenders to manage and run a small airport and this tendering process was governed by strict rules and conditions, one of which was that tenders must be received by the local authority before a strict date and time. The claimants spent time and money preparing a tender and posted it directly into the local authority's own letter box a few hours before the deadline. However, owing to the negligence of the authority, the letterbox was not cleared for 24 hours and when it finally was emptied the claimants' tender was assumed to be late. As a result the tender was not considered by the local authority and the contract was awarded to another tenderer. The question that arose in the case was this. Can the disappointed tenderer bring an action for damages against the local authority for failing to give consideration to its tender?

Before considering the decision in any detail it might be useful to approach this liability question in the abstract, that is to say to look at the precedents as set out in the textbooks and to consider this factual problem from the position of textbook knowledge. Assuming that these facts have not yet reached any court, what would an experienced practitioner or indeed a law academic have made of this liability problem on the basis of the then existing textbook law? Despite the undoubted presence of fault on the part of the local authority, it is not unreasonable to suppose that the practitioner would have had reservations about the chances of liability being imposed on these facts. She might well say that liability would not be imposed in contract because a contract to contract is not a contract (*Courtney v Tolaini* [1975] 1 WLR 297). Equally liability in tort would probably not be imposed given the nature of the damage; there is normally no duty of care for pure economic loss and while there are exceptions to this principle the tendering conditions would probably be interpreted as excluding any duty at the pre-contractual stage (*Caparo Industries plc v Dickman* [1990] 2 AC 605). A negotiating party is not normally under a duty to take into account the interests of the other party (*Walford v Miles* [1992] 2 AC 128).

Yet the local authority was found liable to the claimants and the question arises as to why this was. If the rule of law implies that decisions of the courts will be predictable on the basis of a set of abstract, rationalised and determinable rules and principles is it not a denial of justice to render a decision that seems to contradict these rules and principles?

There is no doubt that counsel for the local authority thought that imposing liability would amount to an injustice. As Bingham LJ noted in his judgment, 'Mr Toulson submitted that the warranty contended for by the club was simply a proposition "tailor-made to produce the desired result" . . . on the facts of this particular case' and that the 'court should not subvert well-understood contractual principles by adopting a woolly pragmatic solution designed to remedy a perceived injustice on the unique facts of this particular case'. Even Bingham LJ, who delivered the principal judgment in favour of the claimants, originally thought that this argument was persuasive. However, what changed his mind were the exchanges with counsel during the hearing. As he states:

During the hearing the questions were raised: what if, in a situation such as the present, the council had opened and thereupon accepted the first tender received, even though the deadline had not expired and other invitees had not yet responded? Or if the council had considered and accepted a tender admittedly received well after the deadline? Mr Toulson answered that although by so acting the council might breach its own standing orders, and might fairly be accused of discreditable conduct, it would not be in breach of any legal obligation because at that stage there would be none to breach (at 1200–1201).

Bingham LJ's reaction to this response was clear:

> This is a conclusion I cannot accept. And if it were accepted there would in
> my view be an unacceptable discrepancy between the law of contract and the
> confident assumptions of commercial parties, both tenderers (as reflected in the
> evidence of Mr Bateson) and invitors (as reflected in the immediate reaction of
> the council when the mishap came to light).

The Lord Justice thus arrives at his conclusion not by applying an abstract
and pre-existing rule to the set of litigation facts but by gradually arriving
at a conclusion through the posing of arguments. It was the responses by
counsel to the judge's questions that convinced him that liability should
be imposed. One might say of this argumentation (dialectical) process
that it was motivated not so much by the formal application of an existing contractual principle, even if technically speaking the Court of Appeal
upheld the trial judge's conclusion that the tendering process on these facts
amounted to a collateral contract. It was motivated more by a functional
argument taking as its starting point the 'confidential assumptions of
commercial parties'. The function of the law of contract is to give effect to
these (reasonable?) assumptions.

This functional approach is then supported by a sleight-of-hand jump
within an apparent description of the facts from a descriptive notion to
a normative concept. Accordingly Bingham LJ follows his commercial
parties' point with a fairly long description of a tendering process to indicate how it is 'heavily weighted in favour of the invitor'. Halfway through
this apparently descriptive paragraph he then says:

> But where, as here, tenders are solicited from selected parties all of them known
> to the invitor, and where a local authority's invitation prescribes a clear, orderly
> and familiar procedure – draft contract conditions available for inspection
> and plainly not open to negotiation, a prescribed common form of tender, the
> supply of envelopes designed to preserve the absolute anonymity of tenderers
> and clearly to identify the tender in question, and an absolute deadline – the
> invitee is in my judgment protected at least to this extent: if he submits a con-
> forming tender before the deadline he is entitled, not as a matter of *mere expec-
> tation* but of *contractual right*, to be sure that his tender will after the deadline
> be opened and considered in conjunction with all other conforming tenders or
> at least that his tender will be considered if others are (at 1202 emphasis added).

And to add extra support to this shift from 'expectation' to 'right' he
reverts to an imaginary oral debate. 'Had the club, before tendering,
inquired of the council whether it could rely on any timely and conforming
tender being considered along with others', he said, 'I feel quite sure that
the answer would have been "of course".' For the 'law would, I think, be

defective if it did not give effect to that'. *Ex facto ius oritur* (law arises out of fact) as a medieval commentator might have put it.

What a case like *Blackpool* illustrates is this. One should perhaps focus less on the perceived substantive law that is seemingly applicable in a liability case and concentrate instead on a variety of fact situations where liability is in issue in order to identify a range of models from which one might be able to see the deployment of different concepts or patterns of concepts and conceptual relations. Thus in the law of tort, liability can be analysed through a number of different conceptual approaches. One might adopt what could be called the descriptive model in which the facts of a tort problem are matched to a set of formal categories of fact situations, themselves set out as a list of 'torts' (and 'torticles') (Rudden, 1991–92). This can be called the causes of action approach and it is descriptive in that one is essentially matching by way of analogy one fact situation with another (See Diplock LJ in *Letang v Cooper* [1965] 1 QB 232, at 242–243). Alternatively one might adopt an interests model whereby the interests of the defendant in any factual situation are matched against those of the claimant (Cane, 1996). This model might be labelled inductive in that one is searching within the facts to induce out of them an apparently descriptive concept ('interest' or 'expectation') in order to transform it into a fully normative concept such as a 'right'. This might well be the best way to characterise the approach used by Bingham LJ in the airport case: he induces out of the facts the notion of an 'expectation' in order to transform it into a 'right'.

However, the appeal judge could equally have adopted some quite different reasoning approaches. He could, for example, have argued that the whole point of a tendering procedure is that it formally establishes at what point there will be a legally binding contract, namely when the invitor accepts a particular tender. Any dealings before this formal acceptance would thus, logically, be subject to the rule that there is no intention to create legal relations. Parties ought to know where they stand in relation to negotiations. Consequently, one might argue, the proper approach is to see law as a set of abstract, or relatively abstract, principles waiting to be applied in a deductive manner. One starts off from the normative proposition – for example 'a contract to contract is not a contract' – and applies it logically to the facts, perhaps employing a dialectical approach to sharpen up the conceptual edge (pre-contract negotiations contrasted with formal acceptance of an offer). Indeed one could take this approach to an even more formal level where the normative propositions (rules and principles) are seen as being analogous to mathematical theorems; precedents and statutory texts are simply the basis for a set of axiomatic propositions (see Gray & Gray, 2003). Rights, within this model, are not induced out of factual situations via the notion of an interest; they exist in a Platonic world of axiomatic legal concepts and relations (see, for example, Hohfeld, 1919).

As we have seen, Bingham LJ did not adopt any of these more formal approaches. He arrived at his conclusion through argument with counsel and through a progressive moving out from one factual situation (ordinary tendering procedure) to another (the extraordinary tendering procedure which formed the facts of the case before him). This indicates that merely studying the common law as a structure of formal rules is inadequate; it fails to embrace the flexibility of different types of reasoning schemes. Logical, functional and structural approaches are different and can lead to different results. Moreover, it is important to note at the outset when analysing a case the remedy being claimed: is it a claim for a debt, for damages, for rescission, for an injunction or for what? In *Blackpool* the claim, as we have seen, was for damages. But imagine that the council had not, when the claimant learned of the fate of its tender, awarded the contract to another tenderer. Could the claimant have obtained an injunction against the council? Could it have brought an action for judicial review? One might finally ask what would have happened if *Blackpool* had been appealed to the House of Lords (now Supreme Court)? Would they have reversed the decision?

4.10   STATUTORY INTERPRETATION

The importance of precedent as a fundamental characteristic of the common law tradition should be treated with caution for another reason. Whatever may have been the position in the past, the primary source of law today in the UK is legislation and this reflects itself in the case-law in that nine out of ten cases heard by the English appeal courts involve the interpretation of a statutory text. In addition to interpreting these public law texts, the courts often have to decide upon the meaning of words or phrases in private texts such as contracts, leases and wills. Traditionally this interpretative function of the courts in common law jurisdictions has given rise to its own set of methods, rules, presumptions and principles. And these are often contained in a different chapter, in books on legal method, from the methods used for handling case-law precedents. These chapters are long and detailed and so only a brief outline can be given about statutory interpretation.

The interpretation of statutes in English law is both a constitutional and a methodological issue. It is constitutional in as much as it is closely tied in with the supremacy of Parliament, which requires that judges apply statutes without any power whatsoever to strike them down as unconstitutional. The judges themselves continue to insist upon this constitutional position even after the coming into force of the Human Rights Act 1998 (*In re K (A Child)* [2001] 2 WLR 1141, para 119). However the judges have reserved to themselves the right to interpret these laws; and it is this reservation that has in part given rise to a number of methodological issues. For example it has encouraged the refusal of the courts, until recently, to look beyond the text itself when it came to interpretation, leading not just to a relatively literal approach to texts (compared with civil law systems) but also to a reluctance to examine Parliamentary reports and debates (see generally *Pepper v Hart* [1993] AC 593). Another factor that has influenced statutory interpretation is history. Before the 19th century statutes were viewed by judges not as statements of principle but as rules governing particularities; they were as a result interpreted strictly and confined to their factual circumstances. Thus the Animals Act 1971, unlike a precedent such as *Rylands v Fletcher* ((1866) LR 1 Ex 265 (Ex); (1868) LR 3 HL 330 (HL)), could never be used as the basis for analogy for a general rule for liability for dangerous things. In turn this attitude has encouraged Parliament to draft detailed texts in a style that is often opaque if not impenetrable. In recent years, however, there has been some modification by the judges with respect to their approach to interpretation.

4.11   RULES OF INTERPRETATION

This change of attitude is not at first sight always obvious to perceive. Thus it has recently been stated that 'it is an elementary rule in the interpretation and the application of statutory provisions that it is to the words of the legislation that attention must primarily be directed'. In other words 'it will be the ordinary meaning of the words which will require to be adopted' and 'whatever the intensity of the process the temptation of substituting other expressions for the words of the statute in the course of interpreting it is to be discouraged, however attractive such a course may seem to be by way of explaining what it is thought the legislature is endeavouring to say' (Lord Clyde in *Murray v Foyle Meats Ltd* [2000] 1 AC 51, 58). This is perhaps an advance on what was once said to be one of the basic rules of English statutory interpretation, namely the literal rule. This rule required judges to follow the words of an Act, if they were clear, 'even though they lead to manifest absurdity' for 'the Court has nothing to do with the question whether the legislator has committed an absurdity' (*R v Judge of the City of London Court* [1892] 1 QB 273, 290). There was, according to this rule, little scope for flexibility (see, for example, *Haigh v*

Charles W Ireland [1973] 3 All ER 1137) and some scope for undermining the intention of Parliament (see, for example, *Fisher v Bell* [1961] 1 QB 394). Accordingly the methodology associated with the literal rule might be termed a 'shallow' hermeneutical approach in that it takes as its point of focus only the text. This restricts of course the type of reasoning and research that can be applied, for the emphasis is on the dictionary and on technical legal concepts rather than the function of the rule. In turn this lack of partnership between judge and legislator has resulted in two textual characteristics. The first is the detailed and often opaque style of legislation and the second is the use of undefined legal concepts. For example s 2(1) of the Misrepresentation Act 1967 is both difficult to read given the long sentences and, anyway, cannot be properly appreciated without a knowledge of the tort of deceit.

This literal approach and method have not disappeared, but there have been developments. Some of these developments are as old as the literal rule itself in as much as this rule was just one of three such approaches. The 'golden' and the 'mischief' rule have long been regarded as alternatives. In addition there has been an important change with respect to external aids: it is now permissible, in certain circumstances, for judges to look at Parliamentary debates in *Hansard* if the statute is ambiguous or obscure (*Pepper v Hart* [1993] AC 593). At a more substantive level, one needs to ask if there have been developments with respect to the type of reasoning used by the judges in statutory interpretation cases.

The first development beyond the literal rule is to be found in a range of 19th-century cases. 'We must . . . in this case', said Jervis CJ, 'have recourse to what is called the golden rule of construction . . . viz., to give the words used by the legislature their plain and natural meaning unless it is manifest from the general scope and intention of the statute injustice and absurdity would result' (*Mattison v Hart* (1854) 14 CB 357, 385). This approach might be said to be an advance on the shallow hermeneutical method in that it does go some way beyond the 'signifier' (words of the text) to embrace a 'signified' that takes its meaning not from the words of the text but the intention of the legislator. However if there is no absurdity then the shallow hermeneutical method applies (see, for example, *Clarke v Kato* [1998] 1 WLR 1647: 'road' does not include car park).

A more profound development, which actually pre-dates the golden rule, is the mischief rule. Lord Diplock has explained its historical context:

> the so-called 'mischief' rule . . . finds its origin in *Heydon's Case*, 3 Co.Rep. 7a decided under the Tudor monarchy in 1584. The rule was propounded by the judges in an age when statutes were drafted in a form very different from that which they assume today. Those who composed the Parliaments of those days were chary of creating exceptions to the common law; and, when they did so,

thought it necessary to incorporate in the statute the reasons which justified the changes in the common law that the statute made. Statutes in the sixteenth century and for long thereafter in addition to the enacting words contained lengthy preambles reciting the particular mischief or defect in the common law that the enacting words were designed to remedy. So, when it was laid down, the 'mischief' rule did not require the court to travel beyond the actual words of the statute itself to identify 'the mischief and defect for which the common law did not provide,' for this would have been stated in the preamble. It was a rule of construction of the actual words appearing in the statute and nothing else.

Lord Diplock then went on to point out that:

> In construing modern statutes which contain no preambles to serve as aids to the construction of enacting words the 'mischief' rule must be used with caution to justify any reference to extraneous documents for this purpose. If the enacting words are plain and unambiguous in themselves there is no need to have recourse to any 'mischief' rule. To speak of mischief and of remedy is to describe the obverse and the reverse of a single coin. The former is that part of the existing law that is changed by the plain words of the Act; the latter is the change that these words made in it (Lord Diplock in *Black-Clawson Ltd. v Papierwerke A.G* [1975] AC 591, 637–638).

Nevertheless, as Lord Nicholls has recently explained, the mischief rule has at least allowed the judges to progress beyond the text through the use of external aids. Nowadays the courts look at external aids for more than merely identifying the mischief the statute is intended to cure and in 'adopting a purposive approach to the interpretation of statutory language, courts seek to identify and give effect to the purpose of the legislation' (*R v Secretary of State for the Environment, Transport and the Regions, Ex p Spath Holme Ltd* [2001] 2 AC 349, 397). Does this mean that the mischief rule has evolved into a functional approach?

Whatever the situation, one can note from Lord Nicholls's comments that the three rules seem to have given way to a rather different method, that of the 'purposive approach'. Other Law Lords have confirmed this method as the contemporary approach (see, for example, Lord Steyn in *R (Quintavalle) v Secretary of State for Health* [2003] 2 WLR 692 para 21). In terms of the three rules, this might be seen as an adoption and extension of the mischief (ie purpose) rule, but care must be taken since 'purpose' probably embraces a policy reasoning aspect that was not at the root of the original mischief rule.

In fact policy can play a more open role in statutory interpretation. In one quite recent case Lord Hoffmann opened his judgment in saying:

> My Lords, on the surface, this does not look like a very momentous case. The question is whether Mr and Mrs Oakley's landlord should have provided them

with a basin in the WC. The statute which they say made it necessary to install one is ambiguous. The language is capable of bearing such a construction. On the other hand, it is very unlikely that this was what Parliament intended. So the courts have a choice. If they say that Mr and Mrs Oakley should have had a basin, landlords of old houses and flats all over the country will have to install them. Local authorities and housing trusts will have to incur very considerable expense. Under the surface, therefore, the case raises a question of great constitutional importance. When it comes to the expenditure of large sums of public and private money, who should make the decision? If the statute is clear, then of course Parliament has already made the decision and the courts merely enforce it. But when the statute is doubtful, should judges decide? Or should they leave the decision to democratically elected councillors or members of Parliament? (*Birmingham CC v Oakley* [2001] 1 AC 617, 628).

The case depended upon how the word 'state' of premises was to be construed and the majority held that this did not cover a bad design which may constitute indirectly a health hazard; they thus distinguished between 'state' and 'layout'. As one of the dissenting judges observed: the 'distinction between layout and state of the premises is not to be found in the statute, and it is certainly not indicated by the language of the provision or the context'. And so it 'is on analysis no more than a verbal technique to cut down the generality of the wording of the modern statute' (Lord Steyn, at 628). However, as we have seen, Lord Hoffmann took the view that if they held the authority criminally liable it would result in local authorities having to spend huge sums of money, an obligation imposed by judges rather than the electorate. As a matter of policy, this was unacceptable.

4.12   HUMAN RIGHTS ACT 1998 AND INTERPRETATION

Another important development with respect to statutory interpretation is to be found in the Human Rights Act 1998. The Act states in s 3(1) that so 'far as it is possible to do so, primary legislation and subordinate legislation must be read and given effect in a way which is compatible with the Convention rights'. The provision undoubtedly gives the judges considerable freedom to adopt a purposive approach and no doubt they are taking advantage of this liberty. Nevertheless it would be a great mistake to think that the literal rule is dead, even as regards constitutional and human rights provisions. In one post-1998 case the Privy Council had to decide if torture was permissible under the Bahamas constitution. Article 17(1) clearly states that no one shall be subject to torture or inhuman treatment or punishment, but article 17(2) goes on to say that this will not apply to any punishment 'that was lawful' before the date of the new constitution.

Astonishingly a majority of the Privy Council held that flogging, admitted by both sides to be torture, was permissible since it was lawful before the said date. As the dissenters pointed out, 'the literal interpretation cannot be the proper interpretation of article 17(2) when due regard is had to its transitional purpose' since such an interpretation 'gives this proviso a wider scope than can have been intended by those who framed and adopted the Constitution'. It 'would deny to citizens the full protection intended to be afforded by article 17(1)' (*Pinder v The Queen* [2003] 1 AC 620, para 69 PC). The majority decision seems astonishing and certainly indicates that the literal approach is not dead. But the House of Lords (now Supreme Court) and Privy Council tend to comprise judges trained for the most part in commercial law and thus an understanding of the more subtle points of public law and basic rights can prove challenging. Perhaps this is the price one pays for not having a specialised constitutional court.

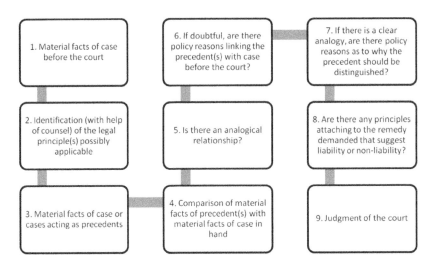

Note: It is not being suggested that all reasoning follows this progression chart; but the chart does set out the kind of steps that might implicitly be followed. Of course the reasoning in the judgments themselves will often focus on an analysis of all the precedents and of the arguments of each counsel and so each progressive step is often hidden behind this discussion and analysis.

Figure 4.1   Case-law reasoning

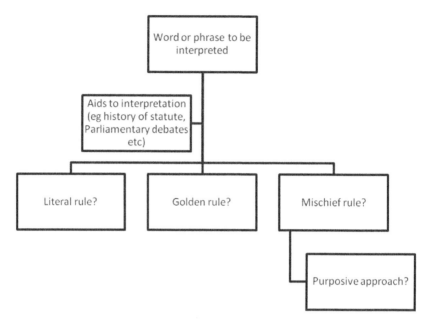

Figure 4.2   Statutory interpretation

5.   English legal education and English legal thought (2): academic theories

Academic writing has also concerned itself, to some extent, with precedent and the notion of the *ratio decidendi* (see generally Cross & Harris, 1991). However rather than focus on what academics have said about precedent – especially as some of the older literature has been absorbed by the judiciary and tends to find expression in their judicial and extrajudicial opinions – it might be more useful to look at case-law reasoning in a wider epistemological context. For theories about case-law as a formal source of law are closely interconnected with theories about law itself and with legal reasoning more generally. The three areas can be usefully brought together under the heading 'epistemology' since they all raise questions about what it is to have legal knowledge (Atias, 1985; 2002). However, before turning to an epistemological consideration of case-law and its methodology something needs to be said about the importance and influence of a number of legal theorists and schools of legal philosophy in the common law world. Some of these theorists will be familiar to many jurists from the civil law tradition, but others will not (see Troper, 2003). And it may be because of the greater impact of certain schools of theory, or indeed individual theorists, on the common law that the conception of 'law' within this tradition turns out to be different than in the civilian tradition. That said, however, there is no doubt that certain ideas have travelled between the two traditions.

5.1   POSITIVISM

One of these ideas that crossed the Channel is positivism. The expression 'positivism', when applied in law, comes from the Latin *ius positum*, which meant posited or laid down law and thus is closely associated with legislation, particularly the codes (see Carbasse, 1998, paras 175–176). In order to understand the impact of this theory one has to recall the ideas that positivism replaced. Before the 19th century the dominant assumption was that there existed a law of nature which in turn assumed dualism in law; there were the civil laws of each individual state (*ius proprium*, *ius positum*) and there was the *ius naturale* which had been identified in Roman law as being the law found in nature (see Stein, 1999, 94–101). Later civilians developed this law of nature into an abstract conceptual system of legal and moral axioms founded on the rational nature of man. The advent of positivism did not as such destroy this abstract and axiomatic view of law (it was seen as legal science instead: Atias, 1994, 96–103); what it destroyed was the idea of dualism. There was no such thing as natural law, only the law posited by each jurisdiction, and thus a 'rule either is or is not law; it cannot at the same time be both'. This led to further assumptions: 'law must be free from contradictions and complete in itself'; and 'law proceeds only from law' so that to 'speak of the law of Nature is to ignore the bounds which the law itself has placed upon its own creative power' (Jones, 1940, 206).

This theory was imported into England by John Austin (1790–1859). He had been a law professor in one of the first faculties of common law in England (although he gave up because of the lack of interest in legal education) but he also spent time in Germany and was much influenced by the Pandectists (on which see Stein, 1999, 119–123). According to Austin, law was a series of 'commands' from political superiors to political inferiors backed up by sanctions. These commands (law) are quite independent of moral rules and to this extent, as Jones has noted, 'Austin was therefore aiming at a "pure" science of law long before the appearance of the school which later adopted the term "pure" as a specific designation for its own teaching' (Jones, 1940, 96). Austin accepted of course that in the common law systems judges made law, but this was because the sovereign had delegated the power to them to do this.

In 1961 was published one of the most influential books on English legal theory ever to appear in the United Kingdom. Herbert Hart's *The Concept of Law* (Hart, 1961) replaced Austin's *The Province of Jurisprudence Determined* (1832) as the foundational text in legal theory and it did this in part by providing a powerful critique of Austin's command thesis. This thesis might to some extent reflect criminal law, but it could not account for whole areas of private law and legal procedure (for example wills) where the command-sanction simply did not accord with reality. Hart consequently distinguished between two categories of rules – primary (direct obligation-imposing) and secondary (power-conferring) – and defined law as a union of these two types of rules. However, from the position of case-law, what is perhaps one of the most important aspects of Hart's thesis is his acceptance of the open texture of law: 'there is a limit, inherent in the nature of language, to the guidance which general language can provide' (1961, 123). Faced with such ambiguity in a rule, a judge has *discretion* in respect of the interpretation and application of the rule. The judge's 'conclusion, even though it may not be arbitrary or irrational, is in effect a choice'. And he continued: 'the criteria of relevance and closeness of resemblance [between a line of cases] depend on many complex factors' and to 'characterize these would be to characterize whatever is specific or peculiar in legal reasoning' (1961, 124). Hart does not, then, provide a theory of legal discretion or legal reasoning as such.

5.2 RETREAT FROM POSITIVISM

This 'failure' of positivism to provide an account of legal reasoning beyond that of choice and discretion left a gap or weakness which has been exploited by other schools and (or) individual theorists. The first of such schools that was to make a major inroad into positivist and conceptual thinking in US law faculties was the school of American Realism which flourished in the 1930s but whose influence is still very much felt today in the common law world ('Realism is dead; we are all realists now': Twining) (see 4.4). The central epistemological theme of Realism is that knowledge of law is not to be found in rules, concepts and so-called logical coherence, but in what the actors in law (policemen, court officials, lawyers, judges etc) actually do. 'What . . . officials do about disputes is', said Karl Llewellyn, 'the law itself' (1951, 12). It was stimulated by the attitude summed up in the words of OW Holmes (an American judge). In asking what constitutes law, he said that you 'will find some text writers telling you that it is . . . a system of reason, that it is a deduction from principles of ethics or admitted axioms or what not'. However, 'if we take the view of our friend the bad man we shall find that he does not care two straws for the axioms or deductions, but that he does want to know what the . . . courts are likely to do in fact' (Holmes, 1897).

However, great care must be taken since the realist school was so wide and diverse that its ideas cannot be reduced to a few propositions. What the realists were doing, in their diverse ways, was reacting against legal formalism and thus they brought into legal knowledge what might generally be termed sociological and psychological dimensions. Predicting how judges would decide a case was not simply a matter of looking at rules and the facts since rules were hopelessly unreliable guides (rule scepticism) and facts utterly elusive and selectively constructed (fact scepticism). It was equally a matter of looking at the social background of the judge and the psychological dimensions of his conduct. Now one important aspect of American Realism is that it was essentially a law school phenomenon; it was a reaction against the 19th-century positivist and conceptualist approach to legal education and one of its most important effects was to shift the emphasis in US law teaching onto case-law and casebooks. This in turn stimulated important reflection and scholarship on the nature of facts in law and upon what motivates judges when it comes to choice and discretion. Another important effect was to destroy the myth that legal rules are certain and that legal solutions and case-law are the result of deductive methodology. There is a body of common lawyers, thanks to Realism, who now regard such formalist and logical thinking as vaguely ridiculous.

Realism was to evolve throughout the 20th century, giving rise to other, more politically or socially radical movements, such as Critical Legal Studies and Feminist Jurisprudence. Critical Legal Studies (CLS) has challenged the idea of law's neutrality and its theorists, unlike the earlier liberal Realists, were more to the left of the political spectrum. Indeed the CLS movement was a reaction against both legal formalism and liberalism and it has undoubtedly left its mark on legal education; yet the extent of its influence in UK faculties is a matter of debate (Cownie, 2004, 53). Feminist Jurisprudence has, and is, proving very challenging as well. However this movement has not operated just at the theory level; it has engaged with central areas of law such as tort and property (Cownie, 2004, 53). Indeed there has been an important contribution to legal reasoning (precedent and statutory interpretation) by Professor Rosemary Hunter who has published a collaborative work which takes some leading English judgements and rewrites them from a feminist perspective (http://www.feministjudgments.org.uk). The book has been endorsed by the United Kingdom's only female Supreme Court justice (in 2012) and thus ought to have some impact on the judiciary (Hunter, McGlynn & Rackley, 2010).

5.3   LAW AND ECONOMICS

Another aspect of Realism is the law and economics school, which sees law as being a reflection of economic interests and, that being the case, the role of judges and legislators is to produce legal solutions that encourage economic efficiency. This movement has certainly left its mark on legal education, but, in addition, it has also made an impact on legal reasoning. Judges sometimes make specific references to economic outcomes and they may well withhold a remedy such as an injunction or specific performance if the granting of such an order would lead to obvious economic inefficiency (see, for example, *Co-operative Insurance Society Ltd v Argyll Stores Ltd* [1998] AC 1). However, as Stephen Waddams points out, it is often not easy to distinguish between reasoning based on principle and reasoning based on (economic) policy. The dichotomy suggests that an area of law like contract – a favourite with the law and economics theorists – can be divided clinically into an 'internal' legal view of the subject based on coherent principle and an 'external' view consisting of economic considerations. Such a dichotomy is in practice very difficult to apply because, when viewed historically, many 'external' considerations have been 'internalised' and incorporated into legal contract knowledge as a matter of principle (Waddams, 2011, 222–223). 'The application of pure principles without any attention to their practical consequences', observes Waddams, 'would bear little resemblance to contract law as it has been' (2011, 223).

The law and economics school is also important in the way the latter discipline appears to provide an empirical 'object' against which law can be measured using a causal analysis. A strictly internal view of law as a body of coherent rules and principles is amenable only to structural and interpretative (hermeneutical) techniques; the system itself can be examined for its coherence and the words of the normative propositions can be analysed for their meaning. Economics permits a different technique. Law can be examined in relation to its economic function and (or) it can be assessed in terms of a causal relationship between, for example, the outcome of cases and the economic environment and efficiency. Indeed this relationship is not confined to micro analysis. Whole legal systems can be tested in terms of their economic efficiency leading to the idea that one 'of the central tenets of comparative law and economics is the idea that there is a competitive market for the supply of law' (Caterina, 2006, 161). Thus for example 'the trust concept has proved to be a very cost-efficient device for certain types of financial transactions, and civilian systems have been under pressure, at the very least, to recognise the existence of the concept' (Ogus, 2007, 162). It has even been suggested that countries adopting legal institutions from the common law tradition experience faster growth than those countries influenced by the civil law (Ogus, 2007, 158), although perhaps one ought to be a little sceptical about this kind of causal analysis. Whatever the situation, an economical analysis of law has a very powerful presence within the common law world.

5.4   RONALD DWORKIN (1931–2013)

Nevertheless it would be quite wrong to think that idealism in the common law world has been completely destroyed by realism. In particular the work of Ronald Dworkin, who succeeded Herbert Hart to the Chair of Jurisprudence at Oxford, is of particular importance because it offers a striking alternative not just to Realism but equally to Hart's vision of law as a system of positive rules in which there are gaps. Just as Hart established his own thesis on the destruction of Austin, so Dworkin built his theories on the dismissal of Hart's vision. Dworkin's contribution to the theory of legal method and reasoning is so striking that it will need to be dealt with in some detail.

Ronald Dworkin's work is of major importance in the common law world, not just because of its own inherent qualities but also because of the reaction it has provoked from his critics. This has given rise to a debate of extraordinary diversity, quality and indeed complexity in the Anglo-American legal and philosophical literature. In terms of philosophy, Dworkin's theories can certainly be regarded as a resurgence of idealism. But in terms of methodology they are hermeneutical in that Dworkin not only sees the role of the judge as being one of interpretation but regards law itself as nothing less than interpretation. From an epistemological standpoint, Dworkin's model gains its 'truth' value from the coherence of its structure. Thus, while a Realist might put the emphasis on the sociological and psychological aspects of judging, Dworkin offers a philosophical theory of this 'doing' based on interpretation by reference to a coherent (rather than correspondence with practice) model of argumentation. It is idealistic rather than empirical in that Dworkin is not claiming (unlike Hart) that his theories are based on an empirical foundation (save perhaps in respect of his analogy with the methods used in literature). He does not on the whole claim that he is describing what judges *actually* do (in the sense that his theories are founded on detailed empirical research); he is asserting how they *ought* to decide cases. One might note, also by way of introduction, that Dworkin's theories, unlike Hart's, are rooted not in a system of positive rules, but in adjudication and he escapes positivism by asserting that judges are interpreting and applying not just rules but equally principles (Dworkin, 1977). These principles may well have sources beyond those formally recognised by the positivists (for example morality).

In one sense Dworkin's work reflects a central idea of the Realists that law is to be found essentially in the cases. However modern realists, now for the most part classified under the CLS, postmodernist and (or) law and economics headings, do not regard Dworkin's theories as providing a satisfactory response to the discretion gap; his theories are too idealistic and (or) ideological (American liberalism). Yet perhaps another of Dworkin's strengths (or weaknesses?) is the relative diversity of his ideas. With respect to adjudication, he does not offer a single thesis; rather, he has propounded a number of different ideas not all of which easily coexist one with another (this is debatable), although they do share the same idealism towards judging and they are all readily accessible given Dworkin's skills of presentation.

5.5   DWORKIN AND HARD CASES

One important distinction made by Anglo-American legal philosophy is between hard and easy cases. 'The term "clear case", writes Bengoetxea, 'refers to a situation of isomorphy in which the applicability of a legal rule or a set of legal rules to certain facts is clear and unproblematic.' And in 'these cases of isomorphy, where the facts of the case clearly fit into the operative facts of the legal rule, which attaches a legal consequence to those facts, judicial action can be accounted for by pointing to the fact that a rule is being almost unreflectively applied' (Bengoetxea, 1993, 184, 186). A hard case is where no valid rule seems to govern the case or there is a choice between two seemingly equally valid rules. Hard cases can also include those cases where a rule appears to govern but leads to undesirable consequences. The rule needs to be interpreted, but it is clear that this will take the interpreter into 'the domain of axiology, morality, or politics and yet legal justification is not expected to question the very system of law nor the ideology of adjudication embodied therein, ie the postulate that legal decisions have to be grounded on legally relevant sources, a postulate that embodies the rule of law ideal . . .' (Bengoetxea, 1993, 146). To the positivist, the hard case is peripheral and results from the open texture of law; law defines itself by reference to the easy case. In contrast the hard case for Dworkin is central to the understanding of law because it raises difficult questions such as that of judicial discretion and of reasoning models.

Dworkin's response to the discretion question is that judges do not have free choice because there is always a right answer to all litigation problems. He bases this thesis on the idea that legal method is one of interpretation and argumentation and that the law itself is a seamless web not just of rules but equally of principles. These principles ensure that there are no gaps in the model; judges are thus always constrained in their act of judging if not by the immediate rule then by the web of principle that exists behind the rules. The existence of this seamless web does not of itself give rise to a right answer but it acts as a general theory within which legal argumentation can take place. Dworkin draws an analogy with an argument about artists. If one asks whether Picasso is a better artist than Racine, Dworkin would reply that it is a bad question because one cannot compare two artists from very different artistic traditions. But to say this requires a general theory of art which holds that art is a response to particular traditions and that it is meaningless to try to compare in terms of quality two artists from two quite different traditions. His non-response is thus supported by the model. However, law is different because its general theory, as envisaged by Dworkin, provides no basis for a non-response of the Picasso and Racine kind. In a hard case it may seem at first sight that two (or more) opposing arguments have equal validity, but one argument will always be superior to another because to deny this is to make a theoretical claim that cannot be supported within the general theory of law itself (as it can in the artists analogy). For, in every case that one studies, there is according to the legal model as envisaged by Dworkin, one argument that turns out to be superior to the others (Dworkin, 1995, 233).

5.6   DWORKIN'S CHAIN NOVEL ANALOGY

Dworkin has taken his interpretative thesis a step further through a striking use of a law and literature perspective. In order to illustrate legal reasoning he has drawn an analogy with the writing of a chain novel. 'In this enterprise', says Dworkin, 'a group of novelists writes a novel *seriatim*; each novelist in the chain interprets the chapters he has been given in order to write a new chapter, which is then added to what the next novelist receives, and so on.' In addition each writer 'has the job of writing his chapter so as to make the novel being constructed the best it can be, and the complexity of this task models the complexity of deciding a hard case under law' (Dworkin, 1986, 229). What Dworkin is pursuing here is the idea of legal reasoning as an interpretative exercise. It is important to note, however, the requirement both of integrity (the requirement to write a novel the best it can be) and of a model of rights and duties themselves founded upon 'the best constructive interpretation of the political structure and legal doctrine of their community' (1986, 255). Thus Dworkin is locating his model very much within a political morality rather than, say, within a model in which the interpreter pursues an economic utility.

One might equally note that the hermeneutical scheme of intelligibility that underpins this literary view of legal reason stands in contrast to the kind of conceptual structuralist model of law fashioned by some positivists in several ways. First, it is not top down in the sense of a pyramid of downward-flowing norms; it is, instead, a more bottom-up approach, which takes as its starting point the judge as author and not the 'rule of recognition' (Hart) or *Grundnorm* (Kelsen) as validator. Secondly, in focusing on the judge Dworkin is really asking a different question than the positivist. Positivists were principally motivated by the question of how a legal norm might be differentiated from other social norms such as those arising out of a moral code. Dworkin, in contrast, was motivated by this question: do judges have discretion? Of course, the positivists, either expressly or implicitly, provide their own answer to this question as we have seen with Herbert Hart. Dworkin set out to challenge the view that, in the hard case, there is such discretion.

Thirdly, Dworkin's hermeneutical theory, while bottom-up in its approach, does nevertheless have something of a structuralist dimension. Dworkin has written that the judge 'must construct a scheme of abstract and concrete principles that provides a coherent justification for all common law precedents and, so far as these are to be justified on principle, constitutional and statutory provisions as well' (Dworkin, 1977, 116–117). What is striking about this last schematic structure is that it is rather similar to the kind of approach advocated by some of the 17th-century natural lawyers. Indeed it even recalls an earlier tradition rooted in the 14th and 15th centuries of a *ius commune* which, like Dworkin's principles, filled the gaps in the *iura propria*. There is, then, a certain paradox to be found in Dworkin's work. In focusing on the judge as author of the law he is undoubtedly a product of the common law case-law tradition; but in advocating a structure of principles where legal and moral norms meet and coalesce he is reintroducing into the common law a theory (or set of theories) that was (were) fashioned by civilians.

5.7 PETER BIRKS (1941–2004)

A jurist who needs to be considered alongside Ronald Dworkin is the late Professor Peter Birks who held the Regius Chair of Civil Law at Oxford. Birks was not a theorist in the sense of being a legal philosopher whose work is treated in books on jurisprudence, but his ideas about legal classification and the importance of Roman law are of relevance in that he was recalling a legal science tradition that was influential in the 19th-century English legal thinking. As we have already mentioned, English law has always been strong on its legal rules but weak on its legal theory and so it has traditionally turned for inspiration to civilian theories which were based on Roman law (Stein, 1980, 123). Of course common law jurisprudence has moved on from these weak days as we have seen. But much of this contemporary legal theory is quite divorced from the kind of taxonomical issues that link traditional legal science with actual positive law. This was a gap that Birks tried to fill. He was not therefore operating at an abstract philosophical level; he was attempting to revitalise legal science (thus Birks makes frequent references to Darwin). And so just as Austin had imported the German Pandectist Roman legal science into English legal thinking, so Birks tried to import the Gaian institutional system.

According to Birks, Gaius was the Darwin of law who had created the institutional scheme which was to be perpetuated and brought into modern Europe by Justinian's *Institutes* (Birks, 1997, 2). This institutional scheme was the basic map of private law which was of universal relevance.

According to Birks, the map would run like this: 'the whole of the law is either public or private; private law is about the persons who bear rights, the rights which they bear, and the procedures by which those rights are realised'. These rights reflect those identified by Roman law scholarship; thus the law of obligations 'is concerned with rights *in personam*' while the law of property 'is concerned with rights *in rem*' (Birks, 1997, 9). Professor Birks then attempted, like others before him, to make English law conform to this map.

5.8   EPISTEMOLOGICAL IMPORTANCE OF THE INSTITUTIONAL PLAN

It has to be said at once that Gaius' institutional plan is of immense importance in the history of legal thought (see Stein, 1999, 18–20). It underpins Western legal thinking and common lawyers cannot escape from its influence (see Chapter 7). In fact what Gaius, a second-century jurist, produced was not so much a plan of the whole of law but a plan of private law. 'All our law', said Gaius, 'relates either to persons, to things or to actions' (G.1.8). In other words a legal system subdivides into three main categories: the law of persons, the law of things and the law of actions. Each of these three subdivisions further divides into sub-subcategories and so the process continues downwards. One should note, however, that the great *summa divisio* between public and private law is not really treated by Gaius in his *Institutes*; this division is asserted by a later jurist, Ulpian (160–223AD), who famously noted that the *ius publicum* is concerned with interests of the state while the *ius privatum* is about private interests (D.1.1.1.2). Thus the plan outlined by Professor Birks is the one to be found in Justinian's *Institutes* (published 533AD), a work that saw itself as a kind of second edition of Gaius.

By modern standards the scheme itself remained somewhat incomplete and it was subsequent European civil lawyers who refined the structure and its contents. Indeed with respect to public law the Romans did little more than supply the actual category and the idea of constitutional and administrative law – public law's two principal subcategories – are on the whole 19th-century creations, although the late medieval jurists did lay the conceptual foundations (see, for example, Canning, 1987). Nevertheless the basic scheme of thought was created by the Roman jurists and although at first sight it might seem somewhat bland, the scheme remains possibly the most important conceptual development ever to be made in legal thought. Professor Birks described it as the 'software' programme for all law.

There is a range of reasons why the scheme is fundamental. First, it was a comprehensive classification of rules. The scheme succeeded in encompassing all private law rules and thus one can take almost any private law rule from any system – including English law – and it can, more or less, be made to fit into this Gaian scheme. Indeed the 18th-century English jurist William Blackstone did just this: his *Commentaries on the Laws of England* is an institutional work.

Secondly, it made a distinction between patrimonial and non-patrimonial rights. Now the point must be made at once that although the Romans did not think in terms of 'rights' as we presently understand the term, the distinction between persons and things represents a difference between laws dealing with 'rights' (*iura*) which attach to people and are inalienable (cannot be sold) and 'rights' attaching to things which are alienable. The distinction thus represents the difference between constitutional and social rights on the one hand and commercial law on the other. An argument today about whether one can sell one's body parts is simply an argument about whether they are patrimonial (things) or non-patrimonial (persons). Moreover certain aspects of the law of persons, such as status, have been attractive categories for English jurists (see Graveson, 1953). In fact there is even an official recognition of the category; status is 'the condition of belonging to a class in society to which the law ascribes peculiar rights and duties, capacities and incapacities' (*The Ampthill Peerage* case [1977] AC 547, 577).

Thirdly, the Gaian scheme was centred on institutions. That is to say the 'person', 'thing' and 'action' are focal points for legal rules in that each exists at one and the same time in the world of fact and the world of law. Thus persons and things are the object of attention by both sociologists and lawyers and consequently they act as the means of moving from the world of fact and reality (for example drivers, cars and victims) to the world of law (legal personality and property). Actions can be seen as having a social reality in courts and enforcement procedures (dispute resolution and remedies). Gaius' scheme therefore represents a bridge between factual reality and law. It is the means by which law attaches itself to social reality and social reality expresses itself in law. However, it is more than just a set of institutions with a real and conceptual existence.

A fourth reason, then, why the Gaian scheme is fundamental to Europe is that it was, and remains, a system. Just as the system of mathematics can create minus numbers, the notion of a thing (*res*) can be extended from a physical thing (*res corporalis*) to an intangible thing (*res incorporalis*). The same is true for a person (*persona*): this can be extended from a physical person to a legal person (corporation), which of course has no physical existence (see Chapter 6). Actions also have their role here. For example, the moment one says that a town can sue in its own right (that is that the town can bring an action), the scheme has effectively turned the town into a 'person', a point seemingly recognised by Gaius himself (D.50.16.16). These developments enabled the construction of a public and a commercial law in later Europe; and they are at the heart of what it is to reason like a lawyer (Samuel, 2002).

Finally, the scheme employed by Gaius was important because it amounted to an exercise of what today we would call scientific reductionism. Gaius himself insists on the importance of generic and specific categories and the need not to confuse them and the use of this scheme allows him to build a conceptually complete ('scientific') structure of law from the basic subdivision of law into three parts down to the lowest and most detailed category. His scheme is not just internally *coherent* but, via the categories of persons, things and actions, all aspects of law are brought together under the single concept of law (*ius*). The later civil lawyers did not have a complete copy of Gaius and thus many of his ideas came into modern Europe through the *Institutes of Justinian* and through extracts preserved in the *Digest* (on which see Stein, 1999, 32–36). The key work was therefore Justinian's rather than Gaius' *Institutes*. However, an almost complete copy of Gaius was discovered in 1816 and there remain in print today translations in several European languages. One might add that this rediscovery of a virtually complete edition permitted Roman law specialists to increase considerably their knowledge of the old law of actions since Gaius, seemingly a bit of a legal historian himself, devotes space to them.

5.9 INSTITUTIONAL PLAN AND ENGLISH LAW

The interesting question of course is the extent to which this plan applies to the common law. Professor Birks thought that it did since he considered that the system transcended Rome to become a scientific structure applicable as a universal 'truth' (or at least until someone came up with a better plan). And there is no doubt that some aspects of English law appear to conform to the categories in the Roman scheme. Thus, for example, constitutional and administrative law make up one of the foundational subjects of the Common Professional Examination, namely Public Law; and three other categories, Property, Obligations I (contract) and Obligations II (tort), seem Roman. In the Roman scheme these three latter categories were part of the law of things, but property and obligations formed the two major subcategories within things and this was reinforced by the principal subdivision in the law of actions between an *actio in rem* and an *actio in personam*. The first action was used to enforce a claim to an item of property based upon ownership and was a remedy aimed at the thing itself. The second was a personal action aimed at another person and based on the existence of a binding obligation described by Justinian as a *vinculum iuris* (legal chain). The paradigm binding obligation was a contract.

At a certain level, then, the common law seems to use Roman categories and subcategories. Yet on closer examination there are problems. The boundaries between the various categories – for example between persons and things and between property and obligations – are by no means watertight. Indeed, in English law, the law of property as a subject area is confined to land law and the distinction between real and moveable (personal) property was not of fundamental importance in the Roman scheme (see Chapter 6). Moreover, in English law, many of the remedies for protecting both real and personal property rights are to be found in the law of tort, which of course is part of the law of obligations (see Chapter 7). In fact English law has no *actio in rem* as such, all 'real' actions having fallen into disuse in the 14th century (see 3.1). The same is true for some 'law of persons' rights; there is often nothing to distinguish a non-patrimonial right from a patrimonial right since most claims sound in the law of tort. For example the remedies for harassment are part of the law of tort and there are even cases that seem to intermix status, contract, property and tort (see, for example, *Stevenson v Beverley Bentinck Ltd* [1976] 1 WLR 483).

In addition to this lack of 'scientific' precision, there is the well-entrenched division between Law and Equity, the latter forming one of the Common Professional Examination categories. Equity is a legal category completely unknown to the civil law systems. This is not to say that civilians have no understanding of the Aristotelian notion of 'equity'; what they do not understand is the rationality of formally distinguishing between two systems of law, namely Common Law and Equity. Thus the idea that a single item of property can be owned at one and the same time by two different people – an owner at common law and an owner in equity (for example the trust) – makes no sense to someone brought up in the Roman tradition because ownership is seen as indivisible (see French Civil Code art 544). The distinction between common law remedies and equitable remedies must seem strange as well (compare with 3.4–5). Another oddity is the idea that one can be the 'owner' of money in another's patrimony (that is to say in another's bank account). It is a fundamental principle of the civil law that money is a consumable item, like bread, and so when handed over to another by way, for example, of a loan, this latter person becomes owner of it. The borrower's liability is simply one sounding in the law of obligations (debt) and not in the law of property. Nevertheless the Court of Chancery was prepared to see trust money fraudulently transferred to a third party as being 'owned' by the trust and thus capable of being 'traced' by the owner (see 3.6: the remedy of tracing).

5.10   MAPPING THE COMMON LAW: SOME OBSERVATIONS

Nevertheless these difficulties do not seem to deter academic lawyers from attempting to apply, from time to time, the Roman institutional scheme to the common law. What was important about the renewed attempt, by Birks, to impose the plan of Justinian's *Institutes* on the common law is that it indicates that at a certain level legal theory is still flirting with Roman legal science. This flirtation is not universally accepted. Jeffrey Hackney has shown how meaningless it is to impose the Roman institutional structure on the old forms of action thinking (Hackney, 1997, 136–138) and Stephen Waddams observes that the 'variety of maps produced since Blackstone's time shows that precision in legal map making has been elusive' (Waddams, 2003, 21). More importantly Waddams' own research into the category and concepts used by courts since Blackstone's time leads him to conclude that 'it has not been possible to explain Anglo-American private law in terms of any single concept, nor has any map, scheme, or diagram proved satisfactory in which the concepts are separated from each other, as on a two-dimensional plane'. Thus a single-minded search for precision in law is likely to be self-defeating (Waddams, 2003, 226, 231).

Yet, as we have said, some academics and indeed even some UK judges continue to flirt with Roman legal science on the basis that the common law lacks taxonomical coherence (see, for example, Descheemaeker, 2009). Reform of the law means reform of the law books. Whatever the merits of this kind of thinking – much of it, arguably, is epistemologically suspect (Samuel, 2000; 2004) – structure and taxonomy has been a topic which brings together legal thought in the civil and the common law. It is an area of legal thought that was once central to 'jurisprudence' but has now been relegated from legal theory to, largely, private law. Legal theory as a subject may have moved well beyond the debates of the 19th century and might reasonably be described as quite forward looking. Debate amongst private lawyers is, in contrast, more backward looking and, as such, is continually drawing on (consciously or unconsciously) the history of the civil law.

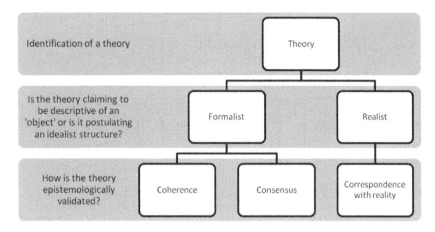

Notes:
1. Realist theories are usually validated, or falsified, through correspondence with an independent object. Thus a theory predicting the appearance of a comet at a particular time will be validated or falsified by its appearance or non-appearance.
2. Formalist or idealist theories often have no independent object as such whose makeup and behaviour is completely independent of the human observer. For example, a theory about the existence or non-existence of God cannot be validated or falsified by reference to an independent object. These theories are dependent upon consensus. If everybody believes in the existence of God, then this acts as a validation.
3. Mathematics is one area of science that cannot be validated by reference to an external object. Mathematical theories are, instead, validated by their internal coherence. If a mathematical theory is found to have an internal contradiction it will be falsified for non-coherence.
4. Many legal theories cannot be validated by reference to an external object. Consequently many are validated by reference to their internal coherence and (or) to their acceptance (consensus) by the majority of jurists.

Figure 5.1   Types of legal theory

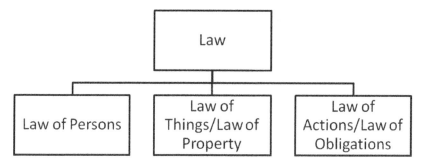

Notes:
1. The original plan employed by Gaius and by Justinian in their *Institutes* was persons, things and actions. The law of things subdivided into property and obligations. However, the later civilian jurists readjusted the plan: they removed actions (to separate codes of procedure) and elevated obligations to take its place. In the *Digest of Justinian* actions and obligations are treated together (D.44.7) and so this is what encouraged the later jurists to make the change.
2. The Law of Persons subdivides into Personality and Status. As marriage is a form of status, family law is treated as part of the Law of Persons. Company law is a question of legal personality and thus is technically part of the Law of Persons.
3. The Law of Property now subdivides into Ownership, Possession and Rights in Another's Property.
4. The Law of Obligations originally subdivided, in Gaius, into Contracts and Delicts but this was found to be (even by Gaius himself) imperfect. He subsequently subdivided obligations into Contracts, Delicts and Various Causes. Justinian modified the plan once again; he subdivided obligations into Contracts, Quasi-contracts, Delicts and Quasi-delicts. This plan has been retained in form in the French Civil Code but the German Civil Code has completely abandoned the 'quasi' categories. The Germans elevated the Roman principle of unjust enrichment into an obligations category with the result that the generally accepted subdivision of obligations in the modern civil law is Contract, Delict and Unjust Enrichment (see generally Samuel, 2010, 2–3, 10–26).

Figure 5.2   Institutional plan (civil law)

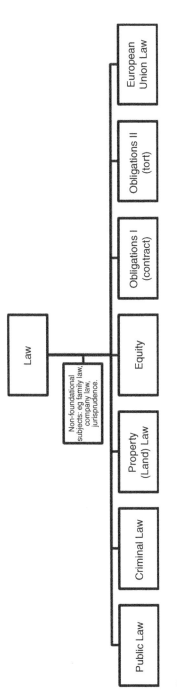

Notes:
1. Non-foundational subjects are usually studied in university law schools alongside the seven foundational subjects. Students who successfully complete the seven foundational subjects (along with a required number of non-foundational subjects) are awarded a qualifying degree which grants them exemption from the first part of the professional examinations.
2. Most English university undergraduate law (LLB or BA Law) students never cover, even in outline, subjects that a civil lawyer would regard as fundamental. Thus very few students ever study civil procedure or moveable (personal) property. Administrative law is usually studied only in outline under Public Law.
3. Most universities have a first-year introductory or general course on law where the court system is studied, but it is perfectly possible for a graduate with both an LLB and an LLM degree to have little or no in-depth knowledge about the UK courts system and its procedures (or its history).
4. Many English law faculties offer comparative law courses or courses on (for example) French or German law (or aspects of these legal systems). Indeed many universities offer, if not joint degrees with a civil law jurisdiction, at least the possibility of studying in a continental law faculty for a term or a year. However, many LLB students will graduate without ever having studied Roman or civil law. Roman law was once required by the English Bar and was, before 1970, widely taught in the universities.

Figure 5.3   Foundational subjects (common law)

6. Legal institutions and concepts in the common law (1): persons and things

Law, as we have seen in the last chapter, is about 'persons', 'things' and 'actions' and this assertion by Gaius remains as true today as it did in the second century AD (see 5.8–10). It has of course been suggested that this institutional model does not impose itself with ease on the common law, but care must be taken here. The common law may not conform to a rigid system (or 'science') which distinguishes public from private law, the law of persons from the law of things, and the law of property from the law of obligations, yet persons, things and remedies remain the fundamental building blocks of the common law. What differs, to continue the building metaphor, is the shape of the building that gets constructed (see 5.9). Consequently any introduction to the common law will need to look at the concepts that it uses in its legal language and its legal reasoning. These concepts, and the categories in which they operate, are also (evidently) of importance in legal education. What are the conceptual building blocks of the common law?

6.1 PERSONS AND THINGS

It is important to appreciate that law is a way of seeing the world. Indeed for many centuries – perhaps right up to the 18th or 19th centuries – law provided a model of institutions and concepts for viewing social and political reality. It was a kind of socio-political model for understanding society. Indeed even today politicians and social scientists can resort to legal notions such as 'contract' and 'property' to describe how people should relate to each other and to the things around them. In the past, legal concepts were, in continental Europe, the only really solid means of providing a social science knowledge framework (Kelley, 1990). In fact there are certain legal relations that were recognised by the Roman jurists which remain highly relevant for all Western lawyers. The importance of 'persons' and 'things' as legal institutions should at once be obvious.

They are objects that exist in society itself and thus they are notions that are equally important to sociologists, political scientists and economists. Consequently persons and things are objects – lawyers call them institutions – by which one can connect the world of law (the world of rules and norms as some would say) to the world of social reality (the acts and behaviour of people and their use of the things around them). This is as true for the common law today as it was for law in Roman times. Moreover, with regard to legal concepts, the common law during the centuries of its development was not afraid to import the language of Roman law (one reason why Latin expressions remained part of the language of the common law until the Woolf reforms).

Yet if law is about the three legal institutions of person, thing and action it means, as the Romans recognised, that law ought to be studied from two different viewpoints. The first viewpoint focuses on the institution itself. What is a 'person'? What is a 'thing'? What is an 'action'? As we shall see, not all persons are 'persons' as far as the law is concerned. Equally there are some 'legal persons' that are not real persons. A similar situation applies to things. What is a 'thing' as far as the law is concerned? Must all 'things' have a physical existence? If not, what intangible things count as property? With respect to actions, one needs to look at all the requirements that attach to an action. If C wants to bring an action against D, what procedures must be followed and what must be proved? In short, one must study persons, things and actions as legal institutions in themselves.

A second viewpoint focuses on the relations between persons and things, persons and persons, and persons and actions. What are these legal relations and what concepts do they generate? For example between person and thing we shall see that there is the important relation of ownership. What is 'ownership'? How can it be acquired and how can it be lost? What are the contents of this notion? Or, put another way, what are the 'rights' that attach to it? Are there, equally, any duties? Between person and person, there are relations such as 'contract' and 'duty of care'. How are these relations formed and discharged? What is their content? Often such existence and content will be dependent on other legal concepts such as 'damage', 'fault' and 'cause'. Yet what amounts to damage, fault and cause in law? Are there some kinds of damage that the law will not actually regard as 'damage'? Are there causal relationships that might exist in the world of fact but are ignored in law? Indeed are there some causal relations that cannot be proved in fact but the law will presume that they exist?

Now these are questions that can only be studied in detailed courses on various areas of the law and thus will not be investigated in any depth in an introductory work (although of course space has been devoted to 'actions': Chapter 3). Nevertheless space should be accorded to persons and things themselves because they, together with actions, are the three building blocks of the whole legal system. However, there is one further institution that must be mentioned because it has given rise to a relationship that is, to a greater or lesser extent (depending on the legal system), independent of the relations between person and thing and person and person. This is the relationship between the individual and the state and forms the basis of public law. It is possible to see the state as a legal subject in itself; that is to say as a special kind of person. Equally it is possible to dispense with the state as a legal institution and focus instead on various entities that make up the state, for example local authorities, ministries and the like. One major difference between the civil law and the common law is that the former does tend to see the state as a juridical 'person' while the common law adopts a more fragmented approach.

6.2   PERSONS

The first basic institution in legal thought is the person: for, as the Romans said, law is constituted for the sake of man (D.1.5.2). A French legal historian suggested that one should adopt a theatre analogy in order to understand how the basic institutions of law functioned; there were actors (persons), props (property) and acting (remedies). This analogy does actually have some connection with the Roman notion of a person in law in that the technical term for a person who could sue and be sued was *persona*, a word that started out as meaning the mask in Greek and Roman theatre. The Romans never developed a theory of *persona* but they certainly recognised that some humans were not *personae* – for example slaves and unborn infants – while some non-human entities, such as colleges or towns, were treated as if they were legal persons. Moreover, within the category of a law of persons (*ius personarum*) two ideas began to emerge. The first is personality, which is concerned with the person as a legal entity. And the second is status, which describes the legal position of a person in society. The distinctions between adults and minors or between citizens and aliens are classical examples of status, but in the past – if not still today – some systems used, or use, status to grant fewer or no rights to certain classes of people within society. The apartheid regime that existed in South Africa before the constitutional revolution remains a prime example; humans were classified into different status categories depending upon the colour of their skin.

Questions of personality are of relevance in all Western legal systems. The human person is the central legal institution to which attach rights and duties and thus the human is the paradigm legal subject. These rights and duties are normally said to be alive as long as the person is alive, but they can extend beyond these limits. In English law many causes of action (rights) and liabilities (duties) are not extinguished with the death of an individual; they vest in the dead person's 'estate' (Law Reform (Miscellaneous Provisions) Act 1934, s 1). If it were otherwise, it would be cheaper to kill a victim than to injure him. As for infants in the womb, they are not as such full legal persons but, as in Roman law (D.1.5.7), a range of interests are protected which may result in a defendant being liable to the child after birth for harm caused before birth (Congenital Disabilities (Civil Liability) Act 1976).

One particularly sensitive issue is death. At what point does a person die? This is by no means an easy question when unconscious – perhaps permanently unconscious – people can be artificially kept alive thanks to technology or when a person disappears without trace. Several practical legal problems arise in this situation. The first, of course, is that determining the time of death can be important both for public and private law and so, to give a very simple example, a person who stabs or shoots a body thinking that the person is still alive will not be guilty of murder if death had in fact arrived before the act. With regard to a person who has disappeared, the relatives will sooner or later want a death certificate so that the presumed dead person's property can be distributed. Secondly, a doctor or a hospital might well want to know, if faced with a permanently unconscious patient, whether or not they are under a duty to keep the body alive by technological means or whatever. In this situation the English courts have developed the test of the 'best interests' of the patient (*Airedale NHS Trust v Bland* [1993] AC 789). If the court determines that it is in the best interests of the person not to be kept alive artificially, it will issue a declaration to the effect that it would not be unlawful to terminate feeding or to switch off the life support machine. All legal systems are faced with serious problems when people disappear and many systems presume death after a certain period of time (often seven years) although a death certificate may be obtained much earlier if there is evidence, for example, that the person missing was involved in some tragedy such as a disappeared aircraft or ship (Presumption of Death Act 2013). But what if, after many years, a presumed dead person reappears? Can he reclaim his distributed property? This was an issue that fascinated medieval Roman lawyers.

6.3   PERSONALITY RIGHTS

Another, more modern, aspect of the law of persons is the question of rights that attach to the person as a person. Civil law systems tend to distinguish between patrimonial and non-patrimonial rights, the first belonging to the law of things (property and obligations) and the second belonging to the law of persons. The actual distinction can be traced back to the French jurist Jean Domat (1625–1696) who identified a group of rights as *jura sua in persona ipso*, that is to say rights which attach to the person himself and consist of the right to life, bodily integrity, liberty and honour. The significance of the distinction is that non-patrimonial rights are not regarded as commercial assets. Accordingly, in addition to those just mentioned, privacy and dignity are not viewed as forms of property but as what might be termed strictly human rights. In French law these two personality rights are thus found in the law of persons section of the *Code civil* rather than the law of things (CC arts 9, 16).

English law certainly recognises a range of rights that the civilian would regard as personality rights. However, until recently it did not classify these within a separate law of persons category. It tended to treat all infringements of such rights as torts, which in the civilian scheme would be part of the law of things. Thus, for example, harassment is a statutory tort (Protection from Harassment Act 1997) and invasions of reputation give rise to the tort of defamation. The situation has changed with the Human Rights Act 1998. Those rights classified as human rights can now be considered as belonging to a category separate from the law of torts and protected by a regime of remedies set out in the 1998 legislation. This does not mean that an invasion of a human right might not also be a tort; but what the legislation has done is to set up a category that could be regarded as essentially one of non-patrimonial rights or rights of personality. Traditionally, then, common lawyers do not normally distinguish between patrimonial and non-patrimonial rights; they tend to treat all invasions of protected interests as if they were valuable assets and thus most torts require proof of damage. There are exceptions – for example defamation – and perhaps these exceptional torts might be seen in terms of being more concerned with personality than property. Yet, whatever the situation in the eyes of the common law, the legislator has now created a separate category of human rights and damages awarded under the legislation are not tort damages (*R (Greenfield) v Secretary of State for the Home Department* [2005] 1 WLR 673, para 19).

6.4   STATUS

Another aspect of the law of persons is status. This, as we have mentioned, is a part of law that deals with a person's legal position in society. It differs from personality in that status is concerned not with defining who is a person; it is about classifying persons into different status groups such as citizen and alien, minor and adult and married and unmarried. One might note here the inclusion of marriage. This at first sight might seem surprising given that marriage is normally regarded as a form of contracting, but it is a form of 'non-patrimonial' contracting, which leads to the creation of the family group. The consequence is that family law is part of the law of persons even if there are fundamental property issues associated with the matrimonial regime.

Status does appear to be a category recognised in English law (Graveson, 1953). This is obviously unsurprising given that distinctions between aliens and citizens and minors and adults are embedded aspects of the law. In fact there is a range of other status groups created by statute that are noteworthy such as the one between prisoners and non-prisoners, the former not having the right to vote in Parliamentary elections. Even within the law of things it is important to recognise certain groups such as 'occupier' and 'visitor', which may be regarded as status groups for some purposes. Thus a 'trespasser' injured on the land of another will not be owed the statutory common duty of care since this duty is owed only to 'visitors' (Occupiers' Liability Act 1957 s 2(1)). In fact one difficulty with respect to such groups is distinguishing status from capacity. Take the following example. A person who buys a motor car can in certain circumstances acquire good title to the vehicle even from a seller who turns out to be a non-owner holding it under a hire-purchase contract. However, this statutory exception will not apply to a 'trade or finance purchaser'. What if a trade or finance purchaser purchases, in his private capacity, a car from a non-owning hirer purchaser? Will he obtain a good title? The answer depends on whether or not the category of a trade or finance purchaser is a status or a capacity category. The Court of Appeal decided that it was a status category and that therefore the statutory exception did not apply; the buyer had the status of a trade or finance purchaser and thus the fact that he bought the car for his private enjoyment (capacity) was irrelevant (*Stevenson v Beverley Bentinck Ltd* [1976] 1 WLR 483).

6.5   LEGAL PERSONS

Legal personality has long been extended beyond the human individual to groups of humans. Thus colleges and towns were on occasions treated 'as if' they were people and in medieval canon law the Church was regarded as a *persona ficta*. In the civil law it was primarily the medieval jurists of the 14th and 15th centuries who developed out of the Roman materials what became known as corporation theory (see, for example, Canning,

1987), this in turn becoming the structural basis for modern public law and modern company law. The expressions used were 'intellectual' (*corpus intellectuale*) or 'moral' person giving rise to the contemporary French expression of *une personne morale* to mean a corporate legal subject.

Some legal systems use legal personality quite widely and even small clubs and associations can register themselves as legal persons capable of having their own patrimony, that is to say fund of assets and liabilities. In England the existence of the trust has meant that the need for legal personality has not been so strong. The trust device permits the establishment of an independent patrimony without formally having to create a legal person. As Maitland said, 'the device of building a wall of trustees enabled us to construct bodies which were not technically corporations and which yet would be sufficiently protected from the assault of individualistic theory' (that is the theory that only individual humans and not corporations exist as realities) (Maitland, 1936, 235). However, early English lawyers developed the idea of a corporation sole which was a device to ensure the continuity of an office, one of the most important of which is the Crown (Crown Proceedings Act 1947). The basic idea of a corporation sole is that the office is deemed separate from the human being holding the office.

These corporations sole are to be distinguished from corporations aggregate, which are collections of individuals organised into a unit which has legal personality and is thus a separate 'person' from the individuals making up the unit. Such a corporation can be established by Royal charter or by statute. The Companies Acts have since the 19th century provided a means by which anyone can create a company by a process of registration; and, once created, the company can, metaphorically, be 'likened to the human body' (*HL Bolton (Engineering) Co Ltd v TJ Graham & Sons Ltd* [1957] 1 QB 159, 172). However, according to English judicial theory this corporate existence is based upon a fiction (*Tesco Supermarkets v Nattrass* [1972] AC 153, 170). The English legal person is thus a *persona ficta*. Nevertheless this has not prevented the judiciary from concluding that such a fictional person can have a real reputation and can thus sue in defamation without having to prove actual damage (*Jameel (Mohammed) v Wall Street Journal* [2007] 1 AC 359).

This idea of an individualised reputation is not the only problem associated with the *persona ficta*. What if an employee of a company causes injury or damage to another person: is it the employee or the company which is directly liable? Companies can find themselves in a direct relationship with another person and so, for example, if one purchases goods which turn out to be defective from a corporate vendor, it is the corporation that will be liable in contract to the buyer. However when a human employee personally causes damage (for example by dangerous driving) liability is normally attributed to the company through a doctrine known as vicarious liability (see 7.5). An employer will be liable for torts committed by an employee acting in the course of his employment. This is a doctrine that does not actually arise out of the law of persons (personality) but out of the law of tort with the result that difficult problems used to arise with the course of employment test when an employee deliberately caused injury to another. The company often became isolated from liability. However, in recent years the courts have alleviated this difficulty by widening the notion of course of employment and so any act that is connected with the employment will often now be sufficient (*Lister v Hesley Hall Ltd* [2002] 1 AC 215).

6.6 UNINCORPORATED GROUPS

Incorporated groups have, then, legal personality and can sue and be sued as if they are people. But what is the position of groups that do not have legal personality? Logically such bodies are not of course 'persons' and so in theory the law of persons endows them with no rights of personality. Nevertheless the law of actions (remedies and procedure) may well permit such groups to bring claims or be sued and indeed partnerships which do not have legal personality can sue or be sued in their own name. Trade unions are another group that does not have legal personality but they are legal subjects thanks to legislation (Trade Union and Labour Relations (Consolidation) Act 1992, s 10 and see also s 127). Departments of government and local authorities are also legal subjects and can thus sue and be sued in their own name, but clubs and the like usually have to have recourse to representative actions (CPR r 19.6(1)).

One particular group that can raise special problems is the family. Margaret Thatcher was reported as saying that there may be 'no such thing as society', but there 'are individual men and women and there are families' (*Women's Own* 31/10/87). If families have a similar real existence as individual humans should the law not take account of this? One difficult and divisive problem is actually defining a family (*Fitzpatrick v Sterling Housing Association Ltd* [2000] 1 AC 27). What are its limits? Does it embrace only a couple and their children or does it extend further? Is it founded (and perhaps confined) to a married couple of opposite sexes or can it consist of a couple of the same sex (see *Fitzpatrick*, above)? The family is certainly an important institution in legal systems and has been in Europe since Roman law. Indeed, as we have mentioned, marriage is not just a contractual relationship but a status and, of course, there are important property issues attaching to the family such as the 'family home'. French law lays down a regime of community property which comes into play upon marriage (CC art 1400 etc) and there are private law duties owed by the spouses to each other. However, in England the starting point of the law is that there are just two individuals subject to the ordinary law of property (*Van den Boogaard v Laumen* [1997] 3 WLR 284, 292–293). This said, there are statutory rights of occupation with regard to the family home (Family Law Act 1996) and the courts have wide statutory powers to adjust property rights between the parties on divorce. The courts have also used the law of remedies to protect, in particular, wives and children. More generally, the law of actions may indirectly take account of the existence of the family (see *Beswick v Beswick* [1966] Ch 538 (CA); [1968] AC 58; *Jackson v Horizon Holidays Ltd* [1975] 1 WLR 1468; *White v Jones* [1995] 2 AC 207).

6.7   FRAGMENTED INTERESTS

Unincorporated associations might not be legal subjects but they are often identifiable units such as a sports club or residents' association. However, there may be a class of people who all have a similar interest in some matter, such as damage suffered by a polluting event or inconvenience resulting from some activity or some act of discrimination. How can their common interest be protected or asserted in a legal action? This is by no means an easy question because the traditional approach of the law is to think in terms of individual persons with individual rights and interests (see Jolowicz, 1983). Group actions are simply not the norm, especially when the interest in question might be too general to be reduced to expression via an individual right.

Nevertheless there are some possibilities. An action may be launched by a particular office holder or public body who has the power to issue proceedings on behalf of a class of persons in order to protect certain interests. For example, a local government can bring actions to protect the interests of local inhabitants (Local Government Act 1972, s 222) and the Office of Fair Trading (OFT) is empowered by various pieces of legislation to seek injunctions to protect certain commercial and (or) consumer interests (see, for example, Unfair Terms in Consumer Contracts Regulations 1999, reg 12). Indeed the OFT has a general enforcement power to protect the 'collective interests of consumers' (Enterprise Act 2002, s 211). Moreover the office of the Attorney-General can be used in a relator action to claim, say, an injunction to restrain a public nuisance (*Att-Gen v PYA Quarries Ltd* [1957] 2 QB 169). Another possibility is a representative action where more than one person has the same interest in a claim (CPR r 19.6(1)). This is the nearest that English law gets to the idea of a class action in which a group sharing a common interest can bring a claim; however, it falls short of a class action in that the requirement of 'the same interest' has been construed quite restrictively (*Emerald Supplies Ltd v British Airways plc* [2011] 2 WLR 203). In addition to the representative action, there is also the group litigation order (CPR r 19.10–11) which is often used to amalgamate claims arising out of a single event such as a serious train accident or illness caused by a dangerous product. This, again, is not a class action as such; it is the amalgamation of claims where there are common or related questions of fact or law.

The general point to be made here is that with regard to collective or fragmented interests the law of persons is often in itself unable to produce a conceptual legal subject capable of vindicating or protecting such interests. Sometimes the legislator will create an office or body to protect a collective interest and when it does this, one can certainly see it as a matter of legal personality in as much as a statutory legal subject is being created. However, in the absence of such a statutory legal person one has to turn, instead, to the law of actions and to rules of procedure. The emphasis is, therefore, on the remedy more than the legal subject and perhaps the more important concept to stress is that of an 'interest' (Jolowicz, 1983). All legal persons have rights, duties and interests; but there are some public and (or) collective interests which cannot be matched to a single legal subject because such a person does not suffer any special or identifiable damage. A good contemporary example of such a collective interest is that of having a healthy and unpolluted environment. The question is one of how such a collective or public interest can be vindicated, especially when the class of persons sharing this interest includes those who have not even been conceived (future generations).

6.8 THINGS

Another way of viewing such an interest is as a 'thing'. Could this interest not be considered as a form of property to be protected using property rather than personality concepts? Everyone has a right to a clean and unpolluted environment just as each person has a right to his or her house, car or other item of property. In fact when several people purchase a single item such as a house or a vehicle one can certainly talk about each individual having a legal 'interest' in the thing. Why should it be different with regard to the environment? Perhaps this is to go too far, but the point to be made is that it provokes one into thinking about 'things' and the law.

Such thinking parallels to some extent the thinking associated with the law of persons. Just as one starts with the physical person, so one starts with the physical thing. However, as the Roman jurist Gaius explained, tangible things (*res corporales*) are things that can be touched (*quae tangi possunt*) such as land, a man, clothes, gold and the like (G.2.13). Gaius then goes on to point out that 'things' (*res*) also encompass intangible things (*res incorporales*) which exist only in law (*quae iure consistunt*) such as a right of way over someone else's land (servitude) or the right to a debt (obligation) (G.2.14). Just as one extended the notion of 'person' to include 'intangible' or 'intellectual' people (*personne morale*) so the *res* could be extended to embrace property created uniquely by the system of law itself ('intellectual' property). Here it is, in effect, the institutional system itself that is creating the *res*.

These intangible forms of property are absolutely fundamental to the modern economic system (Lawson & Rudden, 2002, 29). For example, two of the most common forms of assets are, first, debts and, secondly, copyrights, patents and trademarks. Thus if one had the copyright to all the Beatles records or one was owed several million pounds by a bank one would be a very wealthy person – as wealthy as someone who owned a house, expensive cars and the like. Yet debts and copyrights are not physical at all; they are 'intellectual' in the sense that they are forms of property that are created by the mind rather than by nature so to speak. Indeed, copyrights, patents and trademarks are actually called in law 'intellectual property' (Lawson & Rudden, 2002, 38–43). These forms of property find expression through the legal concept of a 'right'; and so just as one can say that a person has a 'right' to her car or her plot of land one can equally say that one has a right to a debt or in a work of creation such as a piece of music. In the case of intangible things the 'right' becomes the thing itself. Intellectual property is a matter of intellectual property *rights*. Consequently, one can even say that a live performance by a musical group is a form of property provided one puts the emphasis on the 'right' rather than the 'thing' itself (*Ex parte Island Records* [1978] Ch 122). This provokes an important legal question: what amounts to 'property' in the eyes of the law? At a general level the answer seems to be things capable of being *appropriated* (Lawson & Rudden, 2002, 20). So for example the Romans said that a person was not the owner of his or her own limbs (D.9.2.13pr) – although they were quite happy to assert that one person could own another person (slavery) – and public property was deemed incapable of being appropriated by individuals.

Another important aspect of things is one again recognised by the Romans. When is a thing a thing and when is a thing simply a collection of other things? Is a heap of sand a thing? Is a box of nails a thing? Is a flock of sheep a thing? According to the Roman jurists there are three kinds of thing. There is a thing which is unitary in itself ('having a unitary spirit') such as a stone or a wooden beam; there is a thing tightly constructed (cohering) of other things such as a house or a ship; and there are things consisting of other things but given a single name such as a flock of sheep or an army legion (D.41.3.30). The distinctions remain important in relation to the concepts (see below) of ownership and possession. One can obviously own and possess the first category of things and indeed things in the second category; but the third category presents difficulties and the Roman jurists thought that one did not possess, for example, a flock in itself. One possessed only each individual animal. These categories are equally important for the common lawyer. B buys S's house: what is included in the 'thing' (house) sold? Does the sale include, for example, the light bulbs in the light sockets and the fancy coat hooks screwed into the wall?

6.9   CLASSIFICATION OF THINGS

This distinction between things that can be appropriated and things that cannot indicates that the approach of the lawyer towards property is more one of classification than definition. Some things like public property were regarded by the Romans as *res extra commercium*, that is to say outside commercial activity, while others were not. This, of course, was not the only fundamental distinction. The difference between tangible and intangible property, as we have seen, was (and remains) another. However, one fundamental distinction made by the common lawyer is between land and movable property and although this distinction is recognised by civil law systems (see CC art 516) it is not so fundamental in the Romanist thinking. In the common law it is fundamental because land and movable property give rise to two quite different legal regimes. There is a regime dealing with real property (land law) and a regime – or perhaps regimes – dealing with personal property. Within personal property there is an important subdivision between goods, on the one hand, and things in action and money on the other. The buying and selling of goods is subject in part to a specific statutory regime (Sale of Goods Act 1979).

Within the category of goods a sub-distinction that is of particular importance is the one between consumable and non-consumable things. Again this is a distinction that goes back to Roman law. If an owner of a particular book lends it to another, and this borrower refuses to return it, the owner, in any system based on Roman law, has a particular proprietary remedy by which he can reclaim the thing (an *actio in rem*). However if the item lent is a consumable thing – someone 'lends' a bag of sugar or a loaf of bread – the lender cannot obviously ever reclaim the thing itself since it was lent for the borrower to consume and thus the borrow became owner as soon as he received it. All that the lender can do is to claim something equivalent or its value using a personal action (*actio in personam*) (D.12.1.3). The same is true of money in civil law thinking because money is a consumable item (D.7.5.5.1).

The distinction is important in English law as well, but perhaps not in such a fundamental way because, as we shall see, the common law does not have a special action for the recovery of goods. At common law all that a lender has is an action in the tort of conversion for damages against a borrower who refuses to return the borrowed item, but the court can now order the return of the thing itself unless obviously it is a consumable item (Torts (Interference with Goods) Act 1977, s 3). This said, it is still important to distinguish between specific items (a book or a painting for instance) and generic items since the first can be destroyed by accident – thus giving a borrower or bailee (see 3.2) a defence – whereas the second cannot. If a lender lends a loaf of bread the borrower cannot claim that he is not liable for its value because, before being eaten, it was swept away in a flood. The same is true for money; the borrower cannot claim that he is not liable in debt to the lender because he has, after having received the money, lost his job through no fault of his own.

An associated distinction is one between specific and generic goods. One reason why the borrower remains liable for the swept-away loaf of bread is that it is a generic thing. One loaf of bread is no different from another given its consumable nature. Generic consumable goods could not perish and thus the contractual obligation would not be destroyed with the accidental loss of such goods (*genera non pereunt*). Generic goods are not just consumables; a new car, as opposed to a second hand one, is a generic item which does not become specific until it is identified, that is, extracted from stock and put aside for a particular purchaser (*Lazenby Garages Ltd v Wright* [1976] 1 WLR 459).

6.10   RELATIONSHIP WITH THINGS: TWO LEGAL MODELS

From a legal point of view, the most important aspect of property law is the legal relationships that are capable of existing between persons and things. Historically Europe has seen two rather different legal models of these relations. The first is the Roman model that is characterised by a notion of ownership which is founded on the idea of an exclusive power relation between person and thing. This power relation – given expression by the Roman term for ownership, namely *dominium* – was all embracing in that it absorbed every aspect and every interest with respect to the item of property (Patault, 1989, 17). The owner had complete power over the object and this power was not dependent upon anything other than the existence of the relation of ownership. Thus in a claim by a person for the return of his property once the judge had found that the claimant was owner he had to order the defendant to return the object (D.6.1.9).

The second model is the feudal one. This, as we have already noted, made a fundamental distinction between land and movable property (chattels) because the whole structure of a feudal form of government was founded on the grant of land. The king was in theory deemed owner of all the land in his realm and he would then grant large parcels of this land to his lords who swore an oath of loyalty to him by way of contract. In turn these lords would grant smaller parcels to tenants who in turn would grant even smaller parcels to sub-tenants and so on. 'By this process of repeated subinfeudation', writes one English legal historian, 'a chain of tenures was created from the king down to the men who actually occupied the land' (Baker, 2002, 225). The basis of government and power in a feudal society was thus land, status and contract. Now from a law of property point of view, the relationships between people and land were different from the Roman law model. There was not the notion of an exclusive *dominium* between a single person and a single piece of land; several different people had different interests in the same piece of land (Milsom, 1981, 99–101). Thus instead of viewing property relations in terms of an all-embracing relationship between person and physical thing (*res corporalis*) the model was one of a relation between person and an abstract 'interest' in a piece of land, this abstract interest being a form of intangible property (*res incorporalis*) that was related to the status of a person (Patault, 1989, 48–50; Lawson & Rudden, 2002, 79–80).

This feudal model was dominant in Europe in the late Middle Ages but it gradually, though slowly, gave way, in continental Europe, to the Roman model. Indeed the French Revolution was a revolution against the old feudal regime and thus it should be of no surprise that the *Code civil* clearly and firmly re-established the Roman model of property. According to the French Civil Code, 'ownership is the right to enjoy and to dispose of things in the most absolute manner' (CC art 544). As a French writer explained, the importance of this article was that it re-established ownership as a right to a tangible thing rather than just being an intangible right (along with others in the same item of property). The jurists were able to do this because the Romans finally had two synonymous words for ownership, namely *dominium* and *proprietas* (D.41.1.13). This allowed the jurists to merge ownership with the physical thing (*proprietas*, 'property') itself, thus making it a relationship between person and *res corporalis* (Patault, 1989, 219–220). The political implication is that only one individual could be an owner of an item of property.

The English common law was, as we have seen (1.1), originally formed within a strictly feudal regime with the result that English property law still has many characteristics of the feudal model. Whereas the Romanist systems have a single law of property subdivided into ownership, possession and rights in another's property, English law has one regime for land, which still uses feudal concepts (despite the disappearance of feudalism centuries ago), and another for movable property. It even has a third regime for property such as stocks and shares. Moreover, at the level of remedies, it does not recognise any formal division into *in rem* and *in personam* actions. It largely uses the law of tort to protect both real and personal property rights. Nevertheless, while it might be easy to see the feudal model as unduly complex and scholastic when compared to the Roman model, the position is not quite so simple. In the modern world property law also serves as the basis of investment wealth and some 'feudal' ideas – or at least conceptual ways of seeing property – have proved useful. The idea of a strict and all-embracing relation between person and thing might well be ideal when dealing with property as objects, but when dealing with property as wealth the ability to see property rights as abstract interests (*res incorporales*) divorced from the thing itself and capable of being distributed amongst different persons has proved extremely useful (Lawson & Rudden, 2002, 192–200).

6.11 OWNERSHIP

Yet it would be idle to say that the term 'ownership' is not as much embedded in English law as it is in the civil law systems. Certainly as an everyday expression 'ownership' and 'to own' are very familiar expressions both inside and outside legal discourse in English law (see, for example, Consumer Credit Act 1974, s 163; Torts (Interference with Goods) Act 1977, s 6(2): 'true owner'). Yet what exactly is meant when common law lawyers talk of ownership? Given the term's origin in Roman law, one would expect to find one answer in the Roman sources but this proves difficult because the Roman jurists neither defined ownership as such nor did they see it as a 'right' (*jus*). They thus distinguished between having a full power (*plena potestas*) over a thing (J.2.4.4) and rights (*jura*) that others might have in the property (such as a right of way). In other words *dominium* (ownership) and *ius* (right) were separate concepts. But what were the elements of this full power over the thing? It was the late medieval Roman lawyers (the Post-Glossators) who, having trawled the Roman sources for all references to the content of *dominium*, began to see ownership as a *right* (*jus in re*) and to analyse it in terms of its constituent parts, namely a right to use the thing (*ius utendi*), to the fruits of the thing (*ius fruendi*) and to freely dispose of the thing (*ius abutendi*). This was the definition that was readopted by the French Civil Code which, as we have seen, defines ownership as the right to enjoy and dispose of property in the most absolute manner.

The problem with transposing this definition into English law is that the latter has, at least with regard to land, split up the various *iura* into abstract entities in themselves (Lawson & Rudden, 2002, 90–100). Each of them has become an 'estate' or 'interest' capable of being dealt with as an independent entity. Thus

> the beneficial ownership of land may be divided in terms of time as well as space, so that the right to enjoyment of the land for a limited period, such as for life or a term of years, and the right to enjoy land after the expiry of that period, can exist simultaneously as property interests in possession and in remainder or reversion (Lord Hoffmann in *Ingram v IRC* [1999] 2 WLR 90, 93).

Moreover the trust has divided the right to enjoy and the right to dispose of the property between two separate people, the beneficiary and the trustee, each of which are nevertheless said to be 'owners' (one in equity and one at common law). In addition, a contract to possess real property for a term of years – that is to say a lease – is regarded not just as a contract (personal right) but also as a real right that can be bought and sold as property (Law of Property Act 1925, s 1(1)(b)). It is extremely difficult to graft any Roman notion of ownership as an exclusive relationship between person and thing onto this land law structure, although the estate of fee simple in absolute is probably functionally equivalent to ownership. Thus a person in principle has the right to do as he wants on his own land (estate) (*Bradford Corporation v Pickles* [1895] AC 587).

With regard to chattels, the position is seemingly different and that the idea of an exclusive ownership of a thing can be applied with less difficulty than with land. When goods are sold what gets transferred from seller to buyer is 'property' in the goods (Sale of Goods Act 1979, ss 16–18) and this 'property' seems to be ownership, which in turn permits such an owner to dispose of the goods as she wishes. Indeed it has been held that an owner of goods is entitled to be careless with his or her thing provided that such carelessness does not cause physical damage to another (*Moorgate Mercantile Ltd v Twitchings* [1977] AC 890). Yet even with movable property the notion of ownership as a source of legal rights and remedies is not in truth that important. For 'the English law of ownership and possession, unlike that of Roman law, is not a system of identifying absolute entitlement but of priority of entitlement' (Auld LJ in *Waverley BC v Fletcher* [1996] QB 334, at 345). Rather than ownership of property (real or personal), it is more accurate for common lawyers to talk of 'title' to goods or land.

How can ownership (or its nearest equivalent in the common law) be obtained? There are several principal ways: ownership can be acquired by succession (parents leave their house and chattels to their child), by gift, by sale and purchase and by loan when it is a consumable item being loaned. Succession and sale are major areas of substantive law governed by detailed rules; and mention has already been made of the loan of consumable items. However, with regard to sale, two models need to be mentioned. When S sells a piece of property to B the question arises as to when title (ownership) in the property passes from S to B. In Roman law there had to be, in addition to the contract of sale, a conveyance of title; the seller had formally to transfer ownership to the seller and the latter had to accept ownership. This conveyance was a property transaction quite separate from the obligation (contract) transaction, although in the case of sale of goods the conveyance required little formality other than the mental intentions to transfer and to accept together, normally, with a handing over of the goods. German law has adopted this Roman model and so has the English law common law (as opposed to equity) with regard to land. A separate conveyance (now registration at the Land Registry) of the land takes place after exchange of contracts, although the purchaser acquires title to the land in equity on the exchange of contracts and so functionally speaking becomes owner thanks to the contract (Lawson & Rudden, 2002, 59–60).

A second model is one where the contract and conveyance are not separate and it is the contract itself (unless the parties decide differently) that passes ownership or title. This is the model to be found in French law and in English law with respect to goods provided the goods are ascertained (Sale of Goods Act 1979, ss 16–18). One problem with this model is that if the contract turns out to be void (non-existent), then title will not normally pass in English law because no one can give a better title than he or she has (*nemo dat quod non habet*). The consequence is that if the purchaser resells the goods the third party will not get title despite having paid for the goods (see, for example, *Ingram v Little* [1961] 1 QB 31). This problem is avoided in French law thanks to a provision that deems the possessor of a movable item as owner when he sells the goods (CC art 2276). Two dissenting judges in the House of Lords said that this kind of general rule ought to be adopted by English law (see *Shogun Finance Ltd v Hudson* [2004] 1 AC

919). But the position remains that only in limited circumstances will the third party get title to goods purchased from a person who turns out not to have title (for exceptions see, for example, Factors Act 1889). It may be that the status of the person buying the goods will determine whether or not he gets title to them from a seller who has no title (*Stevenson v Beverley Bentinck Ltd* [1976] 1 WLR 483).

6.12 POSSESSION

A second major relation between person and thing is possession. This, as a Roman jurist reminds us, has nothing in common with ownership (D.41.2.12.1), for possession is based on the idea of a factual, rather than a legal, relationship between person and thing (D.4.6.19; D.41.2.3). Possession is the factual control by a person over a thing and can thus exist even when the person is not the owner of the property. The borrower of a book from a library will be in possession of the book while the library remains owner of it. What was, and remains, important about possession as a legal concept is that it was protected by its own particular remedy that was different from the *rei vindicatio* that protected ownership. A dispossessed owner might therefore have two different actions against a wrongful possessor (D.44.2.14.3).

When is a person said to possess goods? According to the Roman jurists what was required to possess was a physical (*corpus*) and a mental (*animus*) control of the thing (D.41.2.3.1; D.41.2.17.1), although physical control was construed quite widely. In fact the Romans never really developed any single principle and there are conflicting statements in the Roman sources as to the actual requirements of this notion. Moreover the Romans also distinguished between possession and detention (*detentio*) of a thing. This distinction was made because there was (and is) in fact an important relationship between possession and ownership; long possession in good faith can result in ownership of the property through prescription or, in English law, as a result of the Limitation Act 1980. In the modern civil law there is no single definition of possession. The Swiss Civil Code defines it as 'one who has control of the thing' (Swiss CC art 919), but the French Civil Code says that it is the 'detention or enjoyment of a thing or a right that we hold or that we exercise ourselves or through another who holds it or who exercises it in our name' (CC art 2228).

What is particularly interesting is the extension by the French to include not just physical objects but also an intangible 'right'. This certainly seems an extension beyond Roman law where it is clearly stated that the property had to be physical (D.41.2.3pr). Yet in later Roman law the idea did begin to emerge that possession was a 'right' or a legal relation (*ius*) as much as a factual one and thus one finds the expression *ius possessionis* in the sources (D.41.2.44pr). The importance of this shift of emphasis from the *res* (thing) to the *ius* (legal relation or right) is that the *ius* itself becomes a kind of *res incorporalis* (intangible thing) and this permits one to talk in terms of possession not just as an existing relationship but as a future relationship (a 'right to possession'). In other words a *ius possessionis* could, like a right to a debt, form part of a person's goods or patrimony (D.41.1.52).

6.13   POSSESSION AND ENGLISH LAW

English law has long made use of the concept of possession partly because this notion reflected more accurately than ownership the relationship between person and land. As Milsom has explained, the relationship between a tenant and his land was founded on a feudal grant known as 'seisin' and like '*possessio* seisin became fundamentally a factual relationship between person and thing' (Milsom, 1981, 119). Given this factual orientation and the absence of any notion of absolute ownership, rights with respect to land were always relative: who, as between two parties, had the better claim? This idea of property rights being a matter of relative title as between two people came to dominate the whole of English property law with the result that it is possession rather than ownership which is the key concept. One should not be surprised by this because, as we have seen, the common law system of remedies was one of personal actions (see 3.1) and so all property disputes were a matter of a personal action by one person against another. If one combines this with the absence of any notion of Roman ownership, the 'most that a person out of possession could claim was a better right to possession than the person in possession' (Baker, 2002, 389). This remains true today. The modern torts of trespass to land and to goods and the tort of conversion do not require the claimant to prove that he or she is 'owner' as such; all that needs to be proved is that the claimant has a better right to possess than the defendant in the action.

As for possession itself, English law has not committed itself to any particular theory. As was observed in one case, it has never worked out a completely logical and exhaustive definition and the word depends upon the context in which it is used (*Towers & Co Ltd v Gray* [1961] 2 QB 351). In commercial law the context may be wider than in criminal law, although much, again, will depend on the facts. Yet there must be some notion of physical control even if this is more abstract on occasions than real and there has equally to be a mental element with regard to the object (see Harris, 1961). It is not easy to imagine a person possessing an object of which he has no knowledge whatsoever – although of course the law might presume such knowledge in a range of situations. The possessor of a piece of land might be deemed to possess everything on the land even if he is unaware of all the objects and the same might be true of the possessor of a cupboard or other container (possessor of the genus is deemed possessor of the species). However, a passenger who found a necklace lying on the ground in an airport terminal and handed it in to the airport authorities was held to have a better right to it than the airport when it was never claimed (*Parker v British Airways Board* [1982] QB 1004). In contrast, a person who trespassed into a local authority public park with a metal detector and found a valuable brooch was held not to have a better right to it than the local authority (*Waverley BC v Fletcher* [1996] QB 334).

At a general level one can sum up by saying this. Despite the various civilian theories based on the formal concepts of *corpus* and *animus*, English law has 'employed possession as a flexible and functional concept, and emphasized different factors in different possessory rules, according to the dictates of justice and social policy' (Harris, 1961, 106). Yet despite this flexibility, the concept is central to English property law. Uninterrupted possession of real property by a non-owner can result in the possessor obtaining ownership (or the best feudal equivalent) thanks to statute (Limitation Act 1980, s 15) and the transfer of possession (but not ownership) in chattels gives rise to a special proprietary relationship called bailment. This bailment relationship is of considerable importance in commercial and consumer law, for all contracts of hire of goods, transport, cleaning and repairing of goods and so on will involve this possessory relationship as well as a contractual one (but one must recall that the 'loan' of a consumable item to be consumed by the borrower will pass ownership in it). Indeed, in commercial law the hire of movable property is linguistically treated as similar to that of a lease of real property; one talks of leasing a car or crane (Lawson & Rudden, 2002, 115–117). Whether or not 'possession is nine tenths of the law' is an interesting question, but possession – and the right to possession – is of immense importance to English lawyers.

6.14 RIGHTS IN ANOTHER'S PROPERTY

Bailment is a good example of a person (the bailee) having a right (possessory) in someone else's thing. Now if the thing (say a motor car) has been transferred to the bailee for repair the bailee will have more than a possessory right to the vehicle: he will have what is called a possessory lien, which will entitle him to keep possession of the vehicle until he is paid for the repairs (*Tappenden v Artus* [1964] 2 QB 185). This is an example of what is called real security – for the creditor has a right not just *in personam* but *in rem* – and there are several different types of such security.

In order to understand the conceptual basis of these real security rights it is probably helpful to look at the stages in which they developed. The basic idea behind real security is that a piece of property acts as the guarantor of a debt and so if the debtor is unable to repay the money owed the creditor can look to the thing in order to recoup his debt. If Roman law is taken as the example, the development of this kind of security went through different stages (Johnston, 1999, 90–95). The first stage was one where the debtor transferred both ownership and possession in the thing acting as security. This of course had two major disadvantages for the debtor; he was deprived of the use of the thing and there was no guarantee that the creditor would retransfer ownership and possession. A second stage was where the debtor transferred only possession in the thing, a contract known as *pignus* or pledge in Roman law. This contract still had the disadvantage that the debtor was deprived of the use of the thing. The final stage was the *hypotheca* or mortgage where the debtor retained both ownership and possession of the thing but the creditor gained a *ius in re* (through being granted an *actio in rem*) in the property (D.20.1.7). Both the pledge and the mortgage have passed into modern law and can be found in English law as well as the civil law.

Mortgages work well enough with respect to land – although the historical development stages were somewhat complex – and are the main method of financing the purchase of houses by most people in England and Wales (Lawson & Rudden, 2002, 141–144). The real right obtained by the mortgage lender is now registered at the Land Registry as a charge on the land acting as security. More complex are mortgages with respect to chattels for the obvious reason that it is extremely difficult to set up any kind of registration system with respect to movable items. Accordingly, while in form chattel mortgages are possible, in practice very restrictive legislation has completely discouraged such a form of security. Nevertheless lawyers have managed to get around the legal difficulties involving chattels by developing the contract of hire purchase and contracts of sale with retention of title (on which see Lawson & Rudden, 2002, 146–148). However pledge remains an important form of chattel real security but of course this involves transferring possession of the goods (bailment) to the pawnbroker.

Another form of real rights are servitudes. Again this is an institution that goes back to Roman law of which there were two kinds. There were those founded on the relationship between person (*persona*) and thing (*res*) – called personal servitudes – and those founded on a relationship between *res* and *res*, called real servitudes. Typical real servitudes were rights of way and rights to channel water over another's land (D.8.3.1) or, in towns, rights to light or to project a roof over another's land (D.8.2.2). These servitudes have passed into the modern civil law and are defined in France as 'a charge imposed upon one piece of land for the usage and the utility of a piece of land belonging to another' (CC art 637). Personal servitudes confer a real right in favour of a person and some of the most important were called usufructs. These were defined as 'a *ius* of using and enjoying the things of another without infraction of the substance of such things' (D.7.1.1). The usufruct applied not just to movable property but were assets in themselves in that they could be bought and sold as forms of intangible property (D.7.1.12.2). Modern civil law defines the usufruct as 'the right to enjoy as owner things of which another has the ownership, but on the condition of conserving the substance of it' (CC art 578). Usufructs can be created in respect of movable property and even consumable items, the owner of the latter right being under an obligation to restore the same quantity and quality of goods (CC art 587).

Servitudes, of which there are two kinds – namely easements and restrictive covenants – have also found their way into English law (Lawson & Rudden, 2002, 153–158). Easements are much like the Roman real servitudes in that they are based on a relationship between two pieces of land (*res* and *res*); the easement – which might be a right of way, a right to light or support of a building – attaches to the dominant tenement and is a burden, so to speak, on the servient tenement. English law also recognises a usufruct but does not call it by this name; it is called a profit and entitles a person to take some profit – for example fish, stones, sand and the like – from land belonging to another. Restrictive covenants are agreements restricting the use of land for the benefit of other land and such agreements attach to (run with) the land rather than just existing as a right between persons. Thus a certain piece of land might have a restrictive covenant prohibiting the building of industrial premises or limiting the range of activities that can be carried out on the property. As the name suggests, such covenants were originally contractual in nature but became real rights in the 19th century; as a result of their *in rem* nature they need to be entered on the Land Register.

6.15 REMEDIES

Many of the English law rights discussed in this chapter are not accompanied by their own specific remedies. This is in contrast to the Roman

model which provided special remedies for protecting ownership, possession and the rights in another's property. Accordingly English law does
not have a set of actions *in rem* and this means that it must look to the
ordinary common law and equitable remedies if there is an infringement
of any law of persons or law of property rights (unless of course there is
a statutory remedy) (see Chapter 3). For example, if one person erects a
structure that invades the property of a neighbour the latter can seek an
injunction (see, for example, *Kelsen v Imperial Tobacco Co* [1957] 2 QB
334). One exception in the area of property law is that the common law can
order repossession of land. However, the other two common law remedies
of debt and damages are not available as free-standing entities; they are
available only if a claimant can show a cause of action. This might not be
difficult if an established real right is infringed; thus the infringement of an
easement will be remedied by an action in private nuisance. But causes of
action have now been categorised into substantive law categories, most
of which are often said to belong in the 'law of obligations'. These causes
of action and obligations will be discussed in the next chapter.

As for equitable remedies like the injunction, this is a general remedy
that is normally available to stop the infringement of any established right
or even on occasions an established interest (see, for example, *Burris v
Azadani* [1995] 1 WLR 1372). And if the court does not wish to grant the
injunction it can always order damages in lieu of an injunction. Invasions
of an intellectual property right often attract the equitable remedy of
account of profits; and the equitable ownership of real property obtained
after the exchange of contracts is enforced by an order of specific performance of the contract (see generally Chapter 3).

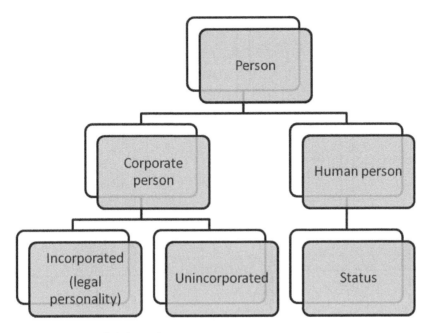

Figure 6.1   English law of persons

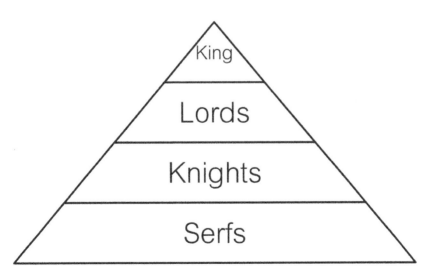

Figure 6.2   Feudal model of law and society

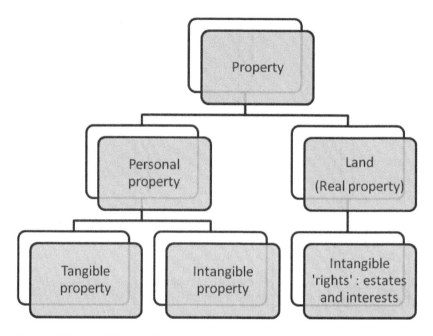

Figure 6.3   Feudal model of property

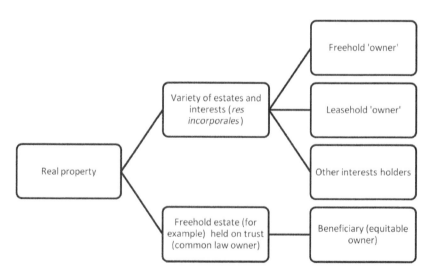

Figure 6.4   Relationship between persons and real property

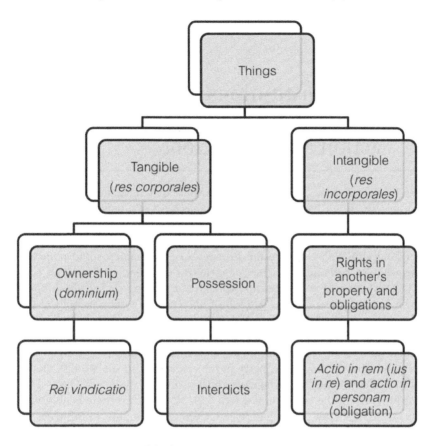

Figure 6.5   Roman model of property

7. Legal institutions and concepts in the common law (2): causes of action and obligations

We have seen how, with the disappearance of real actions in the 14th century, the English common law came to consist of a register of personal actions (Chapter 3). These personal actions, supplemented by remedies developed by the Court of Chancery, remain the basis of liability law in England and Wales. Before the 19th century these actions and remedies themselves largely acted as the categories for classifying the law (see 1.6). However, during the 19th century this situation changed. The abolition of the forms of action and the growth of university law schools opened the door to continental influences with the result that the personal actions – which became causes of action – began to be classified using the language and categories of Roman law. This civilian influence was, as suggested, quite limited; the law of property never succumbed to the Roman model (see Chapter 6) and in consequence the institutional system of Gaius does not properly fit the common law (see 5.9). Nevertheless there is no doubt that the Roman law of obligations has been, and remains, of influence. It is therefore important that the common lawyer knows something about this area of civil law (and see generally Samuel, 2010).

7.1 OBLIGATIONS IN THE CIVIL LAW

The civilian law of obligations has two fundamental formal characteristics. First it is a category that contains rights *in personam* (in Roman law it contained *actiones in personam*), rights *in rem* belonging to the separate category of the law of property (see Chapter 6). Secondly, the category of obligations formed, as we have seen, part of a highly coherent system of private law (see 5.8). Rights *in personam* (personal rights) were defined in part by their opposition to rights *in rem* (real rights) and to personality rights (non-patrimonial rights forming part of the law of persons). However, in addition to these two formal characteristics, the later Roman lawyers actually defined an obligation: an 'obligation is a legal bond (*iuris vinculum*) whereby we are bound by the need to perform something according to the laws of our city' (J.3.13pr). This definition is not particularly helpful as definitions go, but it does have great metaphorical strength in the way it puts the emphasis on the relation (*vinculum*) between person and person. This relationship is, of course, in contrast to the relation between person and thing (property relation).

Gaius in his *Institutes* says that there were two sources ('birth') of obligations, namely contracts and delicts, but at the same time he admits that this duality is inadequate. There are some actions *in personam* that cannot be classified into one or the other of these categories (G.3.91). Thus, in a later work, he adds the third category of 'various causes' (D.44.7.1). This was hardly a satisfactory category for those with a systematic mind and so Justinian in his *Institutes* identifies four sources, namely contracts, quasi-contracts, delicts and quasi-delicts (J.3.13.2). These four categories have found their way into the *Code civil*, although delicts and quasi-delicts are not distinguished; however in the German Civil Code (BGB) both of the 'quasi' categories have been abandoned. Instead of quasi-contracts – which were seemingly justified in Roman law by the principle that 'no one should be unjustly enriched at the expense of another' (D.12.6.14) – there is the category of unjust enrichment (BGB § 812).

Modern civil law books on the law of obligations emphasise the distinction between the obligation as legal bond (*vinculum iuris*) and the various subcategory sources in having a chapter on 'general theory of obligations'. At this level the textbooks discuss, for example, the transmission of obligations and natural obligations, these latter, while giving rise to no actual legal obligation, having certain indirect effects in law. The Romans did not seem very interested in this kind of general theory, but a distinction between obligation and the various types of obligation certainly existed in Roman law. Yet when the Romans talked of obligations in this general way they usually had in mind contractual obligations; in other words a contract was the paradigm obligation (D.5.1.20).

Indeed, even at the level of contract there is not much in Roman law on its generalities since the Romans did not have a general theory of contract. What they had was a law of particular contracts such as sale, hire, partnership, loan and so on. And Ulpian famously observed that a 'bare pact' (*nudum pactum*) – that is to say an agreement that could not be fitted into one of the existing categories (thus lacking *causa*) – would give rise to no obligation (D.2.14.7.4). This said, the Romans did have a general verbal contract called the stipulation, which came into existence as a result of formal words constituting a promise and its acceptance (see G.3.92). In addition Ulpian noted that all the various contracts had the common denomination of agreement (*conventio*) and that there could be no contract and thus no obligation if this was absent (D.2.14.1.3). When this requirement was added to the other Roman requirement of consent (*consensus*: see D.44.7.2) there existed two building blocks upon which a general theory could be erected by the 15th- and 16th-century civilian jurists. The French jurist Jean Domat (1625–1696) thus asserted not just that agreements are formed by mutual consent but that they have the force of legislation between the parties. This view of contract was adopted by the *Code civil* (CC art 1134).

There is one general theory distinction made by the Romans that remains of importance. This is the distinction that obligations arise either *ex contractu* or *ex facto* (D.44.7.25.1). Thus modern civil lawyers talk of obligations arising out of legal acts and obligations arising out of legal facts. The idea of a 'legal act' is in fact broader than just the formation of a contract; it will include, for example, the making of a will and, in German law, the enforceable promise made by a single person. This unilateral promise is thus, in German law, different from contract (*pollicitatio*) (BGB para 657; Draft Common Frame of Reference Bk II, art 4:301). However, in French law such single promises are unilateral contracts (CC art 1103) and this is true of English law as well (*Carlill v Carbolic Smoke Ball Co* [1893] 1 QB 256).

Obligations arising out of 'legal facts' are delicts and quasi-delicts where it is the factual situation itself that generates the obligation. For example if there is an accident in which a person's negligence causes damage to another an obligation will arise in France between the careless person and the victim whereby the former must compensate the latter (CC art 1382). Quasi-contractual obligations also arise out of fact. Where a person receives an enrichment that cannot be justified in law there will be an obligation to repay the enrichment to the person at whose expense the enrichment has been made.

7.2 CONTRACT IN THE COMMON LAW: HISTORICAL DEVELOPMENT

During many centuries the common law remained largely uninfluenced by the categories of the Roman law of obligations. However this does not mean that people were not contracting from the 11th century onwards (or before); undoubtedly they were, and this is why the Court of Chancery developed its remedy of specific performance. What it means is that the common law itself did not at a formal level think in terms of a substantive law of contract based upon agreement and consent. It provided, instead, some remedies when a sale or some other kind of transaction went wrong. For example the unpaid seller of a cow could bring a claim in debt while a buyer who had not received the promised cow could bring an action in detinue. One has to recall that the common law was a series of forms of action (see 1.6). Where there was something of a defect before the 15th century was in the rule that 'not doing is no trespass' which meant that it was difficult to bring a claim for damages against someone who had simply failed to do what he had promised (Ibbetson, 1999, 126–129). However, this was overcome by a species of trespass on the case called *assumpsit*, which by the 17th century had become a form of action permitting a disappointed contractor to obtain damages for breach of a contractual promise (Ibbetson, 1999, 147; Weir, 1992, 1638–1639). Indeed a form of *assumpsit* could even be used for obtaining a debt on the basis that a person who failed to pay was in breach of his promise to repay (although at the level of pleading the debt and damages distinction did not disappear: Ibbetson, 1999, 147–151).

During the 18th century the shape of the modern law of contract began to form thanks in part to the appearance of doctrinal literature, much of it influenced by civilian thinking. In the 19th century a fully formed general theory of contract had established itself in judicial thinking (Atiyah, 1979, 398). Cases were now classified under the category of contract and tort (on which see 7.4) rather than debt, damages, assumpsit and the like (see Bramwell LJ in *Bryant v Herbert* (1877) 3 CPD 389).

7.3   GENERAL THEORY OF CONTRACT

There is no doubt that this general theory had been imported from the civil law (see, for example, the judgment of Lord Coleridge in *Ditcham v Worrall* (1880) 5 CPD 410 and Kekewich J in *Foster v Wheeler* (1887) 36 Ch D 695). As David Ibbetson puts it, one was 'squeezing English rules into models developed elsewhere' (1999, 153). However, despite the talk of contract being founded on 'agreement' this was, and probably remains, inaccurate both as a matter of history and theory. Liability in contract is based on the idea of a breach of promise rather than the non-performance of an agreement. As a House of Lords judge asserted, the 'basic principle which the law of contract seeks to enforce is that a person who makes a promise to another ought to keep his promise'. However, the judge went on to add that this

> basic principle is subject to an historical exception that English law does not give the promisee a remedy for the failure by a promisor to perform his promise unless either the promise was made in a particular form, eg, under seal, or the promisee in return promises to do something for the promisor which he would

not otherwise be obliged to do, ie, gives consideration for the promise (Lord Diplock in *Moschi v Lep Air Services Ltd* [1973] AC 331, 346).

The result is that contract in English law is different from contract in the civil law in several ways. First, it is not formed merely by 'sufficient agreement' (compare with DCFR, Bk II, arts 4: 101–103); there has to be a specific offer and acceptance (*Gibson v Manchester City Council* [1979] 1 WLR 294). Secondly, the existence of a mistake does not prevent a contract being formed; a promise is a promise and only in exceptional circumstances will error make a contract void (*Bell v Lever Brothers* [1932] AC 161). Thirdly, there does not necessarily have to be an 'object' to the promise; as a judge once said:

> If a man covenant, for a valid consideration, that it shall rain to-morrow, he cannot afterwards say, 'I could not make it rain; I did all I could to make it rain; but it would not.' He chooses to covenant that such a thing shall happen, and if it does not, he has broken his covenant (Maule J in *Canham v Barry* (1855) 24 LJCP 100, at 106).

Fourthly, contract itself tends not to be seen as some kind of abstract single binding obligation (*vinculum iuris*) but more as a collection of promises called terms, which are traditionally divided into several kinds. There are express terms – which give rise to problems of interpretation with respect to their language – and there are implied terms, which the courts sometimes have to read into contracts, or a class of contracts, in order to give them efficacy (*The Moorcock* (1889) 14 PD 64). Another dichotomy is the one between conditions and warranties. The former are terms fundamental to the contract which, if broken, will permit the other party not just to claim damages but also to terminate the contract. Warranties are less serious terms which, if broken, give rise only to a claim in damages.

So what is the general theory of English contract law? Lord Diplock expressed it in this way:

> Each promise that a promisor makes to a promisee by entering into a contract with him creates an obligation to perform it owed by the promisor as obligor to the promisee as obligee. If he does not do so voluntarily there are two kinds of remedies which the court can grant to the promisee. It can compel the obligor to pay to the obligee a sum of money to compensate him for the loss that he has sustained as a result of the obligee's failure to perform his obligation. This is the remedy at common law in damages for breach of contract.

Lord Diplock then added:

> But there are some kinds of obligation which the court is able to compel the obligor actually to perform. In some cases . . . a remedy to compel performance by a decree of specific performance or by injunction is also available. It was

formerly obtainable only in a court of equity . . . But, since a court of common law could make and enforce orders for payment of a sum of money, where the obligation was itself an obligation to pay a sum of money, even a court of common law could compel the obligor to perform it (*Moschi v Lep Air Services Ltd* [1973] AC 331, at 346).

Two valuable points arise out of this description. The first is that to talk of damages as the main remedy for breach of contract (as many writers have done) is misleading since such claims are statistically quite rare. By far the most common claim in England and Wales for breach of contract is an action in debt for the price of goods sold, or services supplied, or for unpaid rent or loans. The importance of this statistic is that in substance 90 per cent of all claims in contract are claims for specific performance, that is to say, as Lord Diplock indicated, the claimant is asking the court to enforce directly the defendant's primary obligation (namely to pay a sum of money). Given that debts are a form of intangible property (see 6.8–9) – they are choses in action – contract is really as much part of the law of property as the law of obligations. It is a means by which sellers or suppliers can create property for themselves, although if the debtor goes bankrupt the value of this property might well disappear.

The second point is that, despite the statistical importance of debt claims, the rule that a non-performing contractor is also liable in damages for breach of a contractual promise remains important as a principle of liability. Thanks to the old action of assumpsit, which was a general action for any breach of promise, a breach of contract is a cause of action in itself. All that a claimant who suffers loss or damage has to show is that there was a binding contract between claimant and defendant, that the defendant was in breach of it, that the breach caused the claimant's damage and that the damage was not too remote (*Hadley v Baxendale* (1854) 9 Ex 341; 156 ER 145). And in order for there to be a binding contract, the claimant has to show that there was offer and acceptance, consideration and an intention to create legal relations (*Carlill v Carbolic Smoke Ball Co* [1893] 1 QB 256). In short, once a contract is established, liability to pay a debt or to pay damages attaches to the notion of 'contract' itself. Liability arises out of the breach of the contractual promise (term) broken and not out of facts giving rise to a particular class of contract (for an example of the generality of this cause of action see 4.9).

7.4 TORT

Damages actions that could not be accommodated within the general theory of contract ended up in the category of 'tort' (*Bryant v Herbert*

(1877) 3 CPD 389, 390–391). Accordingly it would be idle to claim that this category has some kind of theoretical underpinning, although there are many academic lawyers who would want to claim otherwise. As Tony Weir put it, tort law 'is what is in the tort books, and the only thing holding it together is their binding' (Weir, 2006, ix). Nevertheless this does not mean that there were not historical developments of importance.

The basis of the modern law of tort is to be found in the writ of trespass and its offshoot, trespass on the case. As David Ibbetson notes, trespass 'lay for invasive interferences to land, goods, or the person' while trespass on the case 'covered a range of situations where the loss had been caused wrongfully' (1999, 154). The distinction between trespass and case was not clearly rationalised for several centuries, but later the difference was expressed in terms of liability based on the invasion of a right and liability based on damage arising from a wrong (Ibbetson, 1999, 155–158). A further development, which had little actual support in legal history, was to be found in the distinction between direct and consequential damage. If the injury had been directly caused by the defendant it was trespass, but if it was indirectly caused it was case (*Scott v Shepherd* (1773) 96 ER 525).

These distinctions are still important today and so trespass will not lie in, say, a pollution case unless the damage was directly caused (see Denning LJ in *Esso Petroleum Ltd v Southport Corporation* [1954] 2 QB 182, 195–196) and the difference between liability based on the invasion of a right and liability based upon a wrong remains an analytical tool (*Three Rivers DC v Bank of England (No 3)* [2003] 2 AC 1, 229). However, the main thrust of development, especially when compared to delictual liability in the civil law, has been the importance of fault as the foundation of liability. Now in the civil law, the modern law of fault liability is founded upon the Roman delict of wrongfully caused damage (*damnum injuria datum*) which, in the later civil law, became the basis for the whole category of delict (see generally Descheemaeker, 2009). This is not to say that strict liability (liability without fault) does not exist; in French law there was a major expansion focused on the *Code civil* article dealing with damage caused by persons and things under the control of another (CC art 1384). But fault became a central moral principle and a means of balancing freedom to act with the causing of damage, an increasingly fraught issue with the industrial revolution. Not surprisingly the same was true of English law: throughout the 18th and early 19th centuries tortious liability became ever more dependent upon the existence of fault (Ibbetson, 1999, 164).

Nevertheless the forms-of-action approach to liability resulted in a situation where the notion of 'fault' did not actually act as a starting point in itself for liability. Thus even in situations where it could be shown that the defendant had intentionally caused damage, there would be no liability unless the claimant went further and indicated a particular category of tort (*Bradford Corporation v Pickles* [1895] AC 587). The claimant had to show the constituents of one of the old forms of action that had become causes of action with the abolition of the forms of action. Thus a claimant had to allege trespass, nuisance, deceit or whatever (*Mogul SS Co v McGregor, Gow & Co* [1892] AC 25; *Esso Petroleum Ltd v Southport Corporation* [1954] 2 QB 182, compare with [1956] AC 218). Even with the development of the tort of negligence, it was not actually the legal fact of carelessness that gave rise to liability. It was the breach of a pre-existing duty of care. Thus, as Ibbetson observes, 'the defining feature of the English (and American) tort of negligence, as compared to its continental equivalents, was the separation between the duty of care and the breach of duty' (1999, 171). In other words liability in the English tort of negligence does not arise, as in French law, out of a legal fact; it arises out of the breach of a pre-existing duty or 'obligation'.

This requirement of a pre-existing duty does bring the tort of negligence quite close to contract in many respects; for the idea of a duty of care had been one of the major contractual implied promises (see now Supply of Goods and Services Act 1982, s 13). In order for there to be liability it must be established that the defendant owed to this particular claimant a duty of care. There has to be some kind of pre-existing obligation between the parties and this was dependent upon the factual notion of proximity. On the other hand there are equally the remnants of a forms-of-action approach in that the duty requirement has allowed the courts to descend from a general principle of negligence to a series of categories of fact situation where duties exist and do not exist. New duties are to be established only by analogy with existing ones (*Caparo Industries plc v Dickman* [1990] 2 AC 605). Thus there is a presumption of no duty when the damage is purely economic or psychological or where the defendant has only failed to act (recalling the 'not doing is no trespass rule'). In addition the forms-of-action mentality is to be found in the fact that negligence is just one, albeit perhaps the most important, tort. There are very many others, all of which are separate causes of action. Thus there are the torts of private nuisance, public nuisance, deceit, defamation, breach of statutory duty, malicious prosecution, misfeasance in public office and liability for animals to name but a few (see Rudden, 1991–92; Samuel, 2010, 181–191).

This means that the category of tort is also significantly different from that of contract. As we have seen, a breach of 'contract' is a cause of action in itself. However, there is no such notion of a 'breach of tort duty' (*Bradford Corporation v Pickles* [1895] AC 587). In order for there to be liability in tort a claimant must show either that the defendant is in breach of a general duty of care owed to him (tort of negligence) or that there exists within the facts a cause of action of some other tort. Nevertheless this formal dimension to the law of tort hides a statistical reality. Just as most contract claims are actions in debt, so most tort claims are actions for personal injury arising primarily out of accidents on the road or in the workplace, although medical negligence claims are beginning to become important as well. Such statistical realities have given rise to the thesis that tort is simply a means of accident compensation and not a very efficient one at that.

Yet tort does have other important roles even if the statistics suggest otherwise. Torts such as trespass to the person (which includes false imprisonment), malicious prosecution, misfeasance in public office and of course negligence have an important public law role. They are the means by which governmental bodies like the police and local authorities can be held to account for their actions. In addition the tort of nuisance can have a role in protecting the environment (*Barr v Biffa Waste Services Ltd* [2012] 3 WLR 795), although statute is diminishing its importance. However, the tort of defamation has perhaps a more negative contribution in the way that it can seriously restrict freedom of speech. This said, defamation can be used to protect certain personality rights such as dignity and even privacy. Tort also provides the remedies for protecting property rights. Trespass to land and trespass to goods are the remedies to be used against those who interfere with possession of property; and conversion is the nearest claim that English law has to a *rei vindicatio* in respect of goods. Intellectual property rights, actually protected for the most part by a statutory regime, are given extra protection by torts such as passing off while the economic torts (for example inducing a breach of contract) protect business interests. The law of tort, in short, provides the remedies for whole areas of the English common law and these remedies are not restricted to damages. The equitable remedy of an injunction can often be used in conjunction with a cause of action in tort to prohibit acts that would invade a personality or property right.

7.5 VICARIOUS LIABILITY AND INSURANCE

In French law, as we have seen, one is liable not only for damage caused through one's own fault but also for damage caused by persons under one's control (CC art 1384). The common law fashioned a very similar principle during the 19th century. However, it has proved very difficult to find any clear theory underpinning the rule that an employer will be liable for torts committed by an employee acting in the course of his or her employment (*Lister v Hesley Hall Ltd* [2002] 1 AC 215, 65). And so, as Ibbetson asserts, because of the lack 'of any principled basis [the rule] rapidly settled down into a set of more or less arbitrary rules' (1999, 182). This said, Lord Phillips has recently made the point that the 'policy objective underlying vicarious liability is to ensure, insofar as it is fair, just and reasonable, that liability for tortious wrong is borne by a defendant with the means to compensate the victim' and that such 'defendants can usually be expected to insure against the risk of such liability, so that this risk is more widely spread' (*Various Claimants v Catholic Child Welfare Society* [2012] 3 WLR 1319, at para 34).

This insurance point is important. Given that the great majority of tort claims are actions for personal injury arising out of accidents on the road and in the workplace, the actual defendants will not be the employer but its insurance company. For insurance is compulsory in both of these situations. Now the relationship between the law of tort and insurance is an ambiguous one in that the law pretends at one level that it does not exist; in the days when there were juries they were not permitted to know if a defendant in an accident case was insured and this attitude has continued even though juries have long disappeared. The court is not supposed to take account of the existence of insurance in allocating liability (*Lister v Romford Ice & Cold Storage Co Ltd* [1957] AC 555). However, this rule seems to break down on occasions (see, for example, *Photo Production Ltd v Securicor* [1980] AC 827) and Lord Phillips appears to be using the existence of insurance as one of the policy reasons not just for justifying vicarious liability but also for extending it beyond the strict employment relationship. As he says, the 'law of vicarious liability is on the move' (*Various Claimants v Catholic Child Welfare Society* [2012] 3 WLR 1319, at para 19).

More generally, there 'is no doubt that insurance profoundly influences the practical operation of the law of tort' (Lewis, 2005, 86). But, this said, the 'real weakness of the insurance argument is that insurance is essentially a group or social phenomenon, whereas the common law of obligations is concerned with individuals' (Cane, 1996, 427). This individualism has resulted in a situation where road accident compensation, in contrast to French law, is still resolutely based on negligent acts rather than the cost of an activity (*Mansfield v Weetabix Ltd* [1998] 1 WLR 1263); and the legislator has done its best to make sure that the same approach is maintained with regard to accidents at work (Compensation Act 2006, s 1). 'There is already concern amongst some of our legislators', said Baroness Hale, 'that the scope for claiming compensation, even for recognised physical injuries, has gone too far' and that 'instead of learning to cope with the inevitable irritations and misfortunes of life, people will look to others to compensate them for all their woes, and those others will then become unduly defensive or protective' (*Majrowski v Guy's and St Thomas' NHS Trust* [2007] 1 AC 224, at para 69). It is not clear whether this 'compensation culture' attitude is actually supported by serious research.

7.6   RESTITUTION (UNJUST ENRICHMENT)

One interesting question that arises out of the relationship between tort and insurance is this. If an insurance company has been paid to take responsibility for a risk such as work injuries, ought such a company to have the right to recover any money paid to an injured employee from, say, the negligent co-employee who injured the victim? That the company has such a right is not in doubt because the remedy of subrogation, as we have seen, allows the insurance company to 'stand in the shoes' of the insured whose damages it has paid and enforce any rights that the insured has against others in respect of the accident (see 3.6). The insurance company can thus sue the negligent employee, via the employer, to recoup its money (*Lister v Romford Ice & Cold Storage Co Ltd* [1957] AC 555). Some tort specialists have argued that this situation results in an unjustified enrichment for the insurance company in that it has been paid to bear a risk that, in the end, it does not have to bear.

However, one problem with talking in terms of the Roman law principle of unjust enrichment is that it was largely excluded thanks to the development of contract and tort in the 19th century, which resulted in a dichotomy that was to dominate English law thinking for well over a century. The dichotomy was this: 'broadly speaking, so far as proceedings *in personam* are concerned, the common law of England really recognises (unlike the Roman law) only actions of two classes, those founded on contract and those founded on tort' (Lord Haldane in *Sinclair v Brougham* [1914] AC 398, 415). This is not to say either that the principle was unknown in English law – it was famously used in one 18th-century case (*Moses v Macferlan* (1760) 97 ER 676) – or that there were not remedies capable of reversing unjustified enrichments. The old actions of debt and account could sometimes fill this role in the past and with the establishment of assumpsit a series of indebitatus assumpsit (in effect debt) claims developed which were quasi-contractual in nature (see Lord Atkin in *United Australia Ltd v Barclays Bank Ltd* [1941] AC 1).

There were three principal quasi-contractual actions, namely the action for money had and received, the action for money paid and the action for payment in respect of services rendered (quantum meruit). Thus, for example, money paid by mistake to the wrong person could be recovered by an action for money had and received and services bestowed on another, if freely accepted, might have to be paid for, thanks to a quantum meruit claim (see, for example, *British Steel Corporation v Cleveland Bridge & Engineering Co Ltd* [1984] 1 All ER 504). Indeed a firm of solicitors was able to recover money which had been embezzled by a partner and gambled away at the defendant's club in an action for money had and received against the casino (*Lipkin Gorman v Karpnale Ltd* [1991] 2 AC 548). Now that gambling contracts are legally enforceable (Gambling Act 2005, s 335) it may be that such a claim would fail today.

The theory originally behind these quasi-contractual claims was that they were based on an implied contract between the claimant and defendant which meant that technically the actions fell within the law of contract and not, as in the civilian systems, into a third category of obligations founded upon the principle of unjust enrichment. After considerable academic pressure in the second half of the 20th century this situation changed and English law abandoned the position that was asserted by Lord Haldane in 1914. There is now a third category of restitution based on the principle of unjust enrichment and this third category is quite separate from both contract and tort (*Kleinwort Benson Ltd v Glasgow CC* [1997] QB 380, 386; [1999] 1 AC 153, 184–185). Moreover, this law of restitution embraces more than just the quasi-contractual claims. It equally includes cases involving equitable remedies such as tracing, founded upon constructive and resulting trusts, account of profits and subrogation. In addition it embraces actions in tort where someone has profited from a wrong. In substance the law of restitution has, technically, extracted from the law of contract all those areas where contracts have turned out to be void or defective in some way but where a party has nevertheless received an enrichment. Whether it has extracted from tort those situations where a person has profited from committing a wrong is less certain given the more fluid character of the 'tort' category.

However, care must be taken with respect to the principle of unjust enrichment itself. It probably has not become a means of directly giving rise to a remedy and thus a claimant will have to show not only that the defendant has received a profit but also that there is an existing cause of action at common law (quasi contract or trespass for example) or in equity which will permit the claim. In fact the principle itself dictates three requirements. The defendant must have received an enrichment at the expense of the claimant which is unjust. Yet what amounts to an enrichment? What amounts to 'unjust'? And what if the enrichment, although unjust, is at no single person's expense? There has been much ink spilled on these questions both in the civil and the common law worlds. Nevertheless one important development that has taken place in more recent times is the expansion of the equitable remedy of account of profits. This action does seem to be becoming something of a general enrichment claim (see, for example, *English v Dedham Vale Properties Ltd* [1978] 1 WLR 93; *Att-Gen v Blake* [2001] 1 AC 268). Whether, however, strict distinctions really need to be made between the law of contract and the law of restitution, given the close relation of the two areas on many issues (for example recovery of money paid pursuant to a defective or frustrated contract), is something that ought not perhaps to worry the courts even if it does worry academics. Unjust enrichment is a principle that can sometimes find expression across the whole of the law of liability.

7.7 STATUTORY CLAIMS

Unjust enrichment has equally had appeal as a political policy. The idea that criminals ought not to be able to enjoy the fruits of their crimes has found expression in a major piece of legislation which has established statutory confiscation and recovery orders for money and property that can be used to extract enrichments arising from unlawful conduct (Proceeds of Crime Act 2002). There is even a provision to trace property (s 305) and to demand an account of profits (s 307). Various other statutes also have restitution provisions. Thus restitution orders can be made for financial services abuses which lead to unjustified enrichments (Financial Services and Markets Act 2000, ss 382–383). Another kind of statutory restitutionary action is one permitting a public authority to reclaim its costs when it has to carry out, for example, remedial work arising from the defendant's act (see, for example, Environmental Protection Act 1990, s 78P). These types of claim for the recovery of costs are debt more than damages actions and are thus restitutionary in form rather than compensatory, which of course distinguishes them from a claim in tort (*Aldora* [1975] QB 748).

However, statutory actions for damages are also available for compensating those who have suffered losses through, for example, the contravention of legislative provisions regarding financial services abuses (see, for example, Financial Services and Markets Act 2000, s 71 and s 150). The Human Rights Act 1998 establishes a damages action (s 8) on behalf of anyone whose human rights have been invaded by a public authority (s 6(1)); and victims of harassment have a statutory civil remedy which includes a right to claim damages (Protection from Harassment Act 1997, s 3). Remedies for intellectual property rights infringements are provided by statute, although the remedies themselves are simply the normal ones supplied by the common law and by equity (Copyright, Designs and Patents Act 1988, s 229). There are many other examples in English legislation of provisions establishing a right to claim damages, compensation, debts, declarations and injunctions. People injured by criminal acts can of course sue the perpetrator if identified in trespass, but there is a statutory compensation scheme covering criminal injuries (Criminal Injuries Compensation Act 1995). However, the scheme only applies to personal injuries. If a victim has suffered just property or financial loss, then, in order to receive compensation, the victim will have to establish tortious behaviour on the part of a government official or body (*Home Office v Dorset Yacht Co* [1970] AC 1004).

7.8 ROLE OF FAULT

The more general role of a principle like unjust enrichment provokes an interesting question. Are there other general principles that emerge from the three categories of the English law of obligations? In his discussion of contractual remedies, Professor Treitel notes that one general requirement in the civil law systems is fault. This 'can be explained on the ground that contract is regarded by these systems as part of the general law of obligations' and thus 'the fault principle which (at least until recently) seemed to be an obvious general requirement in delict was carried over to contract' (Treitel, 1988, 8). Can one say the same of English law? Is fault a general requirement in contract, tort and restitution? The immediate answer is to say that it is not since there are clearly torts such as defamation and damage done by animals where liability is strict. The same is true of contract. Indeed it has been said that in an action for damages for breach of contract 'it is, in general, immaterial why the defendant failed to fulfil his obligations and certainly no defence to plead that he had done his best' (*Raineri v Miles* [1981] AC 1050, 1086).

Nevertheless the position on closer examination turns out to be more complex. In actions for damages for breach of contract much will actually depend upon what is promised. A purchaser damaged by goods not reasonably fit for their purpose or not of satisfactory quality will not have to prove fault in an action against a business seller (Sale of Goods Act 1979, s 14). However, in an action for damages against a supplier of a defective service a lack of care and skill will normally have to be shown (Supply of Goods and Services Act 1982, s 13), although there are exceptions (*Platform Funding Ltd v Bank of Scotland* [2009] QB 426). Moreover, unlike the civilian law rule, the onus might well be on the claimant to prove fault (*Constantine (Joseph) SS Ltd v Imperial Smelting Corporation* [1942] AC 154). Debt claims are normally different; all that the claimant has to show is that the debt is owing. Yet if there is evidence of non-performance by the creditor it could be that this creditor might have to prove that he was not at fault (*Vigers v Cook* [1919] 2 KB 475). More generally it might be asked if contracting parties are not under some general obligation to behave reasonably. The position is by no means clear. All the same, a contractor who behaves abusively may find that the courts have little sympathy (see, for exmple, *Interfoto Picture Library Ltd v Stiletto Visual Programmes Ltd* [1989] QB 433; *Ruxley Electronics Ltd v Forsyth* [1996] 1 AC 344).

As for tort, the establishment of a general duty of care has proved a landmark (*Donoghue v Stevenson* [1932] AC 562). Of course the categories-of-liability approach has by no means disappeared, but it is now overlaid with this duty-of-care concept and so there have been quite subtle trans-formations. Cases that once might have fallen into the category of tres-pass or nuisance now often get treated as just negligence issues; and even some of the old strict liability torts are being injected with an element of fault (see, for example, *Cambridge Water Co v Eastern Counties Leather Plc* [1994] 2 AC 264). One writer has talked of the 'staggering march of negligence' (Weir, 1998). Indeed the House of Lords extended the duty of care concept in one case simply to remedy what the majority in the case perceived to be an injustice that could not be remedied by recourse to the law of contract (*White v Jones* [1995] 2 AC 207). This idea of 'practical justice' suggests that where there is fault that causes a very clear loss the courts might step in, although much depends on the facts and upon policy issues. There is certainly wariness with regard to public bodies, which have been exempted from the duty-of-care principle on many occasions.

In the area of restitution the identification of fault is, at first sight, more difficult. There are some obvious examples such as the profiting from a deliberate wrong. However, in cases where, say, money has been paid by mistake the liability is triggered by the lack of cause for the enrichment rather than by some idea that the defendant has been at fault. Nevertheless the notion of 'unjust' clearly has a fault potential and it may be that some weaker versions of fault can creep in by way of defence. An enriched person who changes his or her position as a result of the payment – for example the payee gives the money to charity or spends it in some other way – might have a defence if it can be shown that the change of position behaviour was reasonable.

None of this means that fault is now a general principle underpinning the whole of contract, tort and restitution. But all the cases might indicate that there is some very general presumption of reasonableness. Such a general presumption is making itself felt in defamation where the idea of the 'reasonable journalist' is beginning to take root (see now *Flood v Times Newspapers Ltd* [2012] 4 All ER 913); and at the level of contract remedies there is a theory of 'efficient breach of contract' which suggests that the courts will be influenced by reasonable economic outcomes (Waddams, 2011, 199–200). Reasonableness, of course, is not always synonymous with fault, although the test for negligence (breach of duty) is whether or not the defendant acted reasonably (*Bolton* v *Stone* [1951] AC 850). It is an expression that can attach as much to outcome as to an individual's behaviour. Is it reasonable that the principle of the law of obligations should be 'no liability without fault'?

7.9   PUBLIC LAW LIABILITY

In France the courts and the legislator have both thought that it is reasonable to abandon the fault principle with regard to certain activities such as motor vehicle accidents. Indeed, not only is there a general liability for damage done by persons under the control of another (vicarious liability), but equally there is liability in respect of damage done by things under the control of a person (CC art 1384). This has given rise to a large area of liability without fault in private law. A strict liability regime has also been developed with regard to administrative liability, that is to say the liability of public bodies and public officials. The foundations of this development are, first, risk attaching to activities that carry dangers for the public and, secondly, the idea that burdens arising from the cost of acting in the public interest should not be borne by individuals. This last principle can be illustrated by the following example. Imagine that the police, in order to recapture a dangerous criminal, have to destroy someone's private property. The equality principle dictates that the state should pay damages to the individual without him having to prove fault because it is not just that the individual should lose his property for the benefit of the community. Put another way the community should compensate the individual for the benefit they have received.

English law, at a formal level, knows no distinction between public and private law. The same law of tort applies to all persons and entities, public or private. Accordingly anyone injured as a result of an activity, even one that carries risk, undertaken by a public body will probably have to prove fault if he or she suffers damage arising from the activity (*Read v J Lyons & Co* [1947] AC 156). The same will be true in the dangerous criminal example; unless fault can be proved the police will not be liable (*Rigby v Chief Constable of Northamptonshire* [1985] 1 WLR 1242). In fact it may be that even if the police are negligent they may be able to escape liability, for policy reasons, on the basis of their public status (see, for example, *Van Colle v Chief Constable of the Hertfordshire Police* [2009] 1 AC 225), thus indicating that in substance – at the level of duty of care – public bodies are sometimes treated differently from private ones. Only if the police commit a trespass might there be liability without fault. If they behave maliciously, on the other hand, there are a number of torts that can come into play.

Is there no principle in English law equivalent to the French equality one? At first sight the answer is clearly a negative one given that there is a decision that turns the French logic on its head. The Court of Appeal have insisted that community benefit means that members of the community should not complain if they occasionally get injured from a dangerous but beneficial activity; they must prove fault (*Dunne v NW Gas Board* [1964] 2 QB 806). Yet more recently a judge has held that individuals ought not to carry the burden of a very noisy military installation; accordingly the tort of nuisance can be used as a means by which the community can compensate these individuals (*Dennis v MOD* [2003] EWHC 793). This perhaps marks an interesting development in English public law liability, although it has to be said that private nuisance has long been a vehicle for ensuring that factory owners who pollute the local environment should pay for this inconvenience (*Bamford v Turnley* (1862) 122 ER 27).

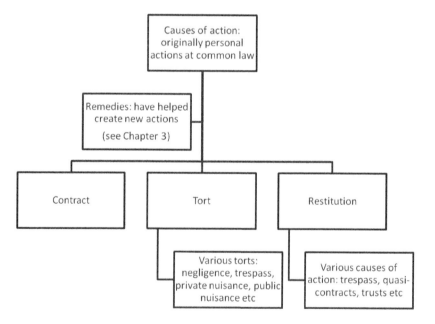

Figure 7.1   Causes of action and their categorisation

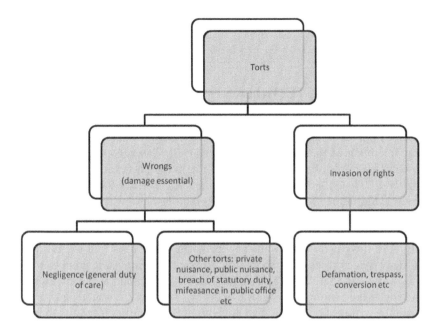

Figure 7.2   Tort(s)

Concluding remarks

One of England's leading legal historians, Sir John Baker, made the point that for much of the common law's history the lawyers 'were trained in advanced schools of municipal law and not in the university law faculties' (Baker, 2003, 12). Perhaps this is the main reason why the common law remained immune to any reception of Roman law and why its institutions owe little to Romano-canonical procedure and its thought patterns seem uninfluenced by Gaius. As we have seen, there was not complete immunity. Yet the royal courts and their procedures were so well established in the early centuries of the common law that the English legal *mentalité* was formed and set at an early stage. This may seem odd to a civil lawyer looking at the common law for the first time. However, it would be wise to recall the words of one of the civil law's great 20th-century legal historians. 'It is amazing and probably unique,' observed Professor van Caenegem, 'that the medieval world suddenly accepted the great law book [*Corpus iuris civilis*] of a society that had been gone for centuries as its ultimate authority and entirely reshaped its own law through scholastic glosses, disputations and commentaries on this venerable relic of a defunct world.' Once seen in this light, 'the English way of developing existing rules, modernising the courts and their procedure and gradually building up new case law or occasionally appealing to the lawgiver, but for the rest letting the professionals get on with their daily task of pleading and adjudicating, appears much more normal' (van Caenegem, 1987, 126). Haphazard in some way, perhaps; but as van Caenegem says, not abnormal.

The common law should not, therefore, be approached as a system that is somehow exceptional in Europe. It should be regarded as the product of actions and facts and not ancient words. This is not to suggest that Roman law and its scholarship proved wanting for modern Europe. Quite the opposite in fact, for while the *Corpus Iuris* was indeed an old book it contained a model that was to prove a challenging and attractive alternative to feudalism. Some, like the late Professor Birks, felt that the common law is still too trapped within a medieval way of thinking and that what is needed is the discipline and rationality of Roman-inspired legal science. Yet others feel, sometimes on economic grounds, that this is misplaced. There is a rugged independence and toughness to English law that makes it attractive to the commercial community. Whatever the situation (and one should not be too seduced by the rhetoric) it would probably be a mistake to suppose that the English common law and the civil law have somehow been converging over the centuries. Certainly there have been influences moving both ways and comparatists are right to point out that one should not put too much stress on the outward appearances of, say, French law (Lasser, 2004). However, there is a different epistemological attitude to law in the two traditions. In the common law the idea of legal science, of a hierarchy of norms and of legal precision and certainty are not really part of the legal mentality. Law is always a matter of argumentation, of dialectics, of reasonableness and practicality, and the way precedents and texts are perceived is as objects to be interpreted and not applied in some mechanistic 'top-down' fashion (*Roxborough v Rothmans of Pall Mall (Australia) Ltd* (2001) 208 CLR 516, 72).

This is not to assert that the common law is 'better' than the civil law. It is not. With respect to the English common law, there are some very serious problems, especially concerning access to justice, and while one cannot fully blame the professional participants themselves, both the professions and the judges have proved wanting on occasions. The cost of legal proceedings is a scandal (see, for example, *Barr v Biffa Waste Services Ltd* [2012] 3 WLR 795) and the lack of strict liability regimes with respect to the two great sources of personal injury, namely vehicle and work accidents, means that insurance companies can usually resist many claims simply on the basis of the costs of suing and the possibility of endless delay. Imaginative judges could have achieved in England what French judges have achieved in France during the 20th century with respect to liability without fault. However, they have done little to reform the law of tort and have even reasserted the primacy of fault in traffic accident cases (*Mansfield v Weetabix Ltd* [1998] 1 WLR 1263). As for procedure, Lord Woolf with the help of the legislature has tried to tackle the problem, but it is likely that any success will be limited, at least when it comes to the cost of litigation. What is worse is that the legislature has now abandoned the civil process. There will soon be virtually no legal aid for civil cases and the conditional fee arrangement could be modified which will limit even further access to the courts. Civil lawyers are likely to have little respect for a system that seems uninterested in providing a service for the majority of its citizens. Perhaps one positive procedural factor is that a litigant is not forced to use the services of lawyers; yet the litigant in person will create as many problems for the system as it solves. Another positive factor is that Alternative Dispute Resolution is being taken increasingly seriously, although some regard ADR as inferior justice if not worse.

Whatever the criticisms, the common law ought not to be taught in isolation from the civil law tradition. Whole aspects of the common law – procedure, taxonomy, the hierarchy of the courts, ADR and so on – ought to be learned and reflected upon in a comparative context which will bring out the characteristic elements of each tradition. One can describe the trial process with its emphasis on an oral tradition, but the characteristics become so much sharper when a student appreciates that a French or a German lawyer may see and do things differently. Comparison can also provoke reflection on some of the English common law institutions themselves. Why are there two levels of appeal courts, particularly after many centuries of English courts without any true court of appeal? Are tribunals quite different legal institutions than courts? Is an English law trial a fundamentally different way of resolving a dispute than the French *procès*? Would the United Kingdom benefit from a genuine constitutional court similar to the German or French one? And if there were to be a constitutional court, could it help solve access to justice problems? Many other questions of a similar kind can be posed. They cannot, and have not, been tackled in this introductory book, but they do indicate that knowledge of a legal system goes much further than merely acquiring a descriptive knowledge of courts, procedures, remedies, judges, professionals and so on in a particular country.

Bibliography

Andrews, N (2000), A New Civil Procedure Code for England: Part Control (2000) 19 *Civil Justice Quarterly* 19

Atias, C (1985), *Épistémologie juridique* (Presses Universitaires de France, 1985)

Atias, C (1994), *Épistémologie du droit* (Presses Universitaires de France, 1994)

Atias, C (2002), *Épistémologie juridique* (Dalloz, 2002)

Atiyah, P (1979), *The Rise and Fall of Freedom of Contract* (Oxford University Press, 1979)

Austin, J (1832), *Province of Jurisprudence Determined* (John Murray, 1832, reprinted Cambridge University Press, 1995)

Baker, J (2002), *An Introduction to English Legal History* (Butterworths, 4th edn, 2002)

Baker, J (2003), *The Oxford History of the Laws of England: Volume VI 1483–1558* (Oxford University Press, 2003)

Beatson, J & Zimmermann, R (2004), *Jurists Uprooted: German-speaking Émigré Lawyers in Twentieth-century Britain* (Oxford University Press, 2004)

Bell, J (1983), *Policy Arguments in Judicial Decisions* (Oxford University Press, 1983)

Bell, J (2006), *Judiciaries within Europe: A Comparative Review* (Cambridge University Press, 2006)

Bengoetxea, J (1993), *The Legal Reasoning of the European Court of Justice* (Oxford University Press, 1993)

Berman, H (1983), *Law and Revolution: The Formation of the Western Legal Tradition* (Harvard University Press, 1983)

Birks, P (ed) (1997), *The Classification of Obligations* (Oxford University Press, 1997)

Birks, P (1997a), Definition and Division: A Meditation on *Institutes* 3.13, in Birks (1997) 1

Birks, P (1998), The Academic and the Practitioner (1998) 8 *Legal Studies* 397

Blomeyer, A (1980), Types of Relief Available (Judicial Remedies), *International Encyclopedia of Comparative Law*, Volume XVI, Chapter 4 (JCB Mohr) (completed 1980)

Boyron, S (2010), La *summa divisio* vue d'outre-Manche, in B Bonnet & P Deumier (eds), *De l'intérêt de la summa divisio droit public-droit privé?* (Dalloz, 2010) 121

Cairns, J (1984), Blackstone, An English Institutist: Legal Literature and the Rise of the Nation State (1984) 4 *Oxford Journal of Legal Studies* 318

Cane, P (1996), *Tort Law and Economic Interests* (Oxford University Press, 2nd edn, 1996)

Cane, P & Stapleton, J (eds) 1998, *The Law of Obligations: Essays in Celebration of John Fleming* (Oxford University Press, 1998)

Canning, J (1987), *The Political Thought of Baldus de Ubaldis* (Cambridge University Press, 1987)

Cappelletti, M (1989), *The Judicial Process in Comparative Perspective* (Oxford University Press, 1989)

Cappelletti, M & Garth, B (1986), Introduction – Policies, Trends and Ideas in Civil Procedure, *International Encyclopedia of Comparative Law*, Volume XVI, Chapter 1 (JCB Mohr) (completed 1986)

Carbasse, J-M (1998), *Introduction historique au droit* (Presses Universitaires de France, 1998)

Caterina, R (2006), Comparative Law and Economics, in Smits (2006) 161

Cohen, F (1935), Transcendental Nonsense and the Functional Approach (1935) 35 *Columbia Law Review* 809

Cownie, F (2004), *Legal Academics* (Hart, 2004)

Cownie, F & Cocks, R (2009), *'A Great and Noble Occupation': The History of the Society of Legal Scholars* (Hart, 2009)

Cross, R & Harris, J (1991), *Precedent in English Law* (Oxford University Press, 4th edn, 1991)

Darbyshire, P (2011), *Darbyshire on the English Legal System* (Sweet & Maxwell, 10th edn, 2011)

Davies, ACL (2008), *The Public Law of Government Contracts* (Oxford University Press, 2008)

Descheemaeker, E (2009), *The Division of Wrongs: A Historical Comparative Study* (Oxford University Press, 2009)

Dworkin, R (1977), *Taking Rights Seriously* (Duckworth, 1977)

Dworkin, R (1985), *A Matter of Principle* (Oxford University Press, 1985)

Dworkin, R (1986), *Law's Empire* (Fontana, 1986)

Dworkin, R (1995), Y a-t-il une bonne réponse en matière d'interprétation juridique, in P Amselek (ed), *Interprétation et droit* (Bruylant/Presses Universitaires d'Aix-Marseille, 1995) 227

Fiss, OM (1984), Against Settlement (1984) 93 *Yale Law Journal* 1073

Gaius, see Gordon & Robinson (1988)

Galeotti, S (1954), *The Judicial Control of Public Authorities in England and in Italy* (Stevens & Sons, 1954)

Garde, R (1841), *An Analysis of the First Principles, or Elementary Rules, of Pleading* (Maxwell, 2nd edn, 1841)

Goff, R (1983), 'The Search for Principle', reprinted in W Swadling and G Jones (eds) (1999), *The Search for Principle: Essays in Honour of Lord Goff of Chieveley* (Oxford University Press, 1999) 313

Gordon, W & Robinson, O (1988), *The Institutes of Gaius* (Duckworth, 1988)

Graveson, R (1953), *Status in the Common Law* (Athlone, 1953)

Gray, K & Gray, S (2003), The Rhetoric of Reality, in J Getzler (ed), *Rationalizing Property, Equity and Trusts* (Butterworths, 2003) 204

Guest, A (ed) (1961), *Oxford Essays in Jurisprudence* (Oxford University Press, 1961)

Hackney, J (1997), More than a Trace of the Old Philosophy, in Birks (1997) 123

Harris, DR (1961), The Concept of Possession in English Law, in Guest (1961) 69

Hart, H (1961), *The Concept of Law* (Oxford University Press, 1961)

Hazeltine, HD, Lapsley, G & Winfield, PH (eds) (1936), *Maitland Selected Essays* (Cambridge University Press, 1936)

Hedley, S (1999), How has the Common Law Survived the 20th Century? (1999) 50 *Northern Ireland Legal Quarterly* 283

Herzog, P & Karlen, D (1977), Attacks on Judicial Decisions, *International Encyclopedia of Comparative Law*, Volume XVI, Chapter 8 (JCB Mohr) (completed 1977)

Hohfeld, W (1919) *Fundamental Legal Conceptions* (Yale University Press, 1919; reprint, 1966)

Holland, TE (1924), *The Elements of Jurisprudence* (Oxford University Press, 13th edn, 1924)

Holmes, OW (1897), The Path of the Law (1897) 10 *Harvard Law Review* 457

Hunter, R, McGlynn, C & Rackley, E (2010), *Feminist Judgments: From Theory to Practice* (Hart, 2010)

Ibbetson, D (1999), *A Historical Introduction to the Law of Obligations* (Oxford University Press, 1999)

Jamin, C (2012), *La cuisine du droit* (Lextenso éditions, 2012)

Jestaz, P & Jamin C (2004), *La doctrine* (Dalloz, 2004)

Johnston, D (1999), *Roman Law in Context* (Cambridge University Press, 1999)

Jolowicz, HF (1963), *Lectures on Jurisprudence* (Athlone, 1963)

Jolowicz, JA (1983), Protection of Diffuse, Fragmented and Collective Interests in Civil Litigation: English Law (1983) *Cambridge Law Journal* 222

Jolowicz, JA (1985), Public Interest and Private Damage (1985) *Cambridge Law Journal* 370

Jolowicz, JA (ed) (1992), *Droit anglais* (Dalloz, 2nd edn, 1992)

Jolowicz, JA (1992), Les appels civils en Angleterre et au Pays de Galles [1992] *Revue Internationale de Droit Comparé* 355

Jolowicz, JA (1996), The Woolf Report and the Adversary System (1996) 15 *Civil Justice Quarterly* 198

Jolowicz, JA (2003), Adversarial and Inquisitorial Models of Civil Procedure (2003) 52 *International and Comparative Law Quarterly* 281

Jones, J (1940), *Historical Introduction to the Theory of Law* (Oxford University Press, 1940)

Kelley, D (1990), *The Human Measure: Social Thought in the Western Legal Tradition* (Harvard University Press, 1990)

Kirby, M (2007), Judicial Dissent – Common Law and Civil Law Traditions (2007) 123 *Law Quarterly Review* 379

Kohl, A (1982), Romanist Legal Systems, in *International Encyclopedia of Comparative Law*, Volume XVI, Chapter 6, Part II (JCB Mohr) (completed 1982)

Lasser, M (1995), Judicial (Self-)Portraits: Judicial Discourse in the French Legal System (1995) 104 *Yale Law Journal* 1325

Lasser, M (2004), *Judicial Deliberations: A Comparative Analysis of Judicial Transparency and Legitimacy* (Oxford University Press, 2004)

Lawson, F (1980), *Remedies of English Law* (Butterworths, 2nd edn, 1980)

Lawson, F & Rudden, B (2002), *The Law of Property* (Oxford University Press, 3rd edn, 2002)

Legrand, P (1996), European Legal Systems are not Converging (1996) 45 *International and Comparative Law Quarterly* 52

Legrand, P & Samuel, G (2008), *Introduction au* common law (La Découverte, 2008) (*Repères n° 514*)

Lewis, R (2005), Insurance and the Tort System (2005) 25 *Legal Studies* 85

Llewellyn, K (1951), *The Bramble Bush* (Oceana, 1951)

Lloyd, D (Lord) & Freeman, M (2008), *Lloyd's Introduction to Jurisprudence* (Sweet & Maxwell, 8th edn, 2008)

Lobban, M (1991), *The Common Law and English Jurisprudence 1760–1850* (Oxford University Press, 1991)

Maitland, FW (1936), see Hazeltine, Lapsley & Winfield (1936)

McCrudden, C (2006), Legal Research and the Social Sciences (2006) 122 *Law Quarterly Review* 632

Milsom, S (1981), *Historical Foundations of the Common Law* (Butterworths, 2nd edn, 1981)

Mommsen, T, Krueger, P & Watson, A (1985), *The Digest of Justinian* (University of Pennsylvania Press, 1985) (4 vols)

Moréteau, O (2000), *Droit anglais des affaires* (Dalloz, 2000)

Munday, R (2002) 'All for One and One for All': The Rise to Prominence of the Composite Judgement in the Civil Division of the Court of Appeal (2002) *Cambridge Law Journal* 321

Ogus, A (2007), The Economic Approach: Competition Between Legal Systems, in Örücü & Nelken (2007) 155

Oliver, D (2001), Pourquoi n'y a-t-il pas vraiment de distinction entre droit public et droit privé en Angleterre? (2001) *Revue Internationale de Droit Comparé* 327

Örücü, E & Nelken, D (eds) (2007), *Comparative Law: A Handbook* (Hart, 2007)

Patault, A-M (1989), *Introduction historique au droit des biens* (Presses Universitaires de France, 1989)

Perrot, R (2010), *Institutions judiciaires* (Montchrestien, 14th edn, 2010)

Roberts, S & Palmer, M (2005), *Dispute Processes: ADR and the Primary Forms of Decision-Making* (Cambridge University Press, 2005)

Rochfeld, J (2011), *Les grandes notions du droit privé* (Presses Universitaires de France, 2011)

Rudden, B (1991–92), Torticles (1991–92) 6/7 *Tulane Civil Law Forum* 105

Samuel, G (2000), Can Gaius Really be Compared to Darwin? (2000) 49 *International & Comparative Law Quarterly* 297–329

Samuel, G (2002), Comparative Law and the Legal Mind, in P Birks & A Pretto (eds), *Themes in Comparative Law in Honour of Bernard Rudden* (Oxford University Press, 2002) 35

Samuel, G (2003), *Epistemology and Method in Law* (Ashgate, 2003)

Samuel, G (2004), English Private Law: Old and New Thinking in the Taxonomy Debate (2004) 24 *Oxford Journal of Legal Studies* 335–362

Samuel, G (2005), Can the Common Law be Mapped? (2005) 55 *University of Toronto Law Journal* 271

Samuel, G (2007), *Contract Law: Cases and Materials* (Sweet & Maxwell, 2007)

Samuel, G (2007a), Civil Codes and the Restructuring of the Common Law, in D Fairgrieve (ed), *The Influence of the French Civil Code on the Common Law and Beyond* (British Institute of International and Comparative Law, 2007) 91

Samuel, G (2008), *Tort: Cases and Materials* (Sweet & Maxwell, 2nd edn, 2008)

Samuel, G (2010), *Law of Obligations* (Edward Elgar, 2010)

Samuel, G (2011), La collégialité et les juridictions anglaises, in F Hourquebie (ed), *Principe de collégialité et cultures judiciaires* (Bruylant, 2011) 179

Smits, JM (2006), *Elgar Encyclopedia of Comparative Law* (Edward Elgar, 2006)

Spencer, J (1998), *La procédure pénale anglaise* (Presses Universitaires de France, 1998)

Stein, P (1980), *Legal Evolution: The Story of an Idea* (Cambridge University Press, 1980)

Stein, P (1984), *Legal Institutions: The Development of Dispute Settlement* (Butterworths, 1984)

Stein, P (1999), *Roman Law in European History* (Cambridge, 1999)

Sutton, R (1929), *Personal Actions at Common Law* (Butterworths & Co, 1929)

Swadling, W & Jones, G (eds) (1999), *The Search for Principle: Essays in Honour of Lord Goff of Chieveley* (Oxford University Press, 1999)

Treitel, G (1988), *Remedies for Breach of Contract* (Oxford University Press, 1988)

Troper, M (2003), *La philosophie du droit* (Presses Universitaires de France, 2003)

Twining, W (1973), *Karl Llewellyn and the Realist Movement* (Weidenfeld & Nicolson, 1973; reprint 1985)

Ullmann, W (1975), *Medieval Political Thought* (Penguin, 1975)

van Caenegem, R (1971), History of European Civil Procedure, *International Encyclopedia of Comparative Law*, Volume XVI, Chapter 2 (JCB Mohr) (completed 1971)

van Caenegem, R (1987), *Judges, Legislators and Professors: Chapters in European Legal History* (Cambridge University Press, 1987)

van Caenegem, R (1992), *An Historical Introduction to Private Law* (Cambridge University Press, 1992)

van Caenegem, R (1995), *An Historical Introduction to Western Constitutional Law* (Cambridge University Press, 1995)

van Caenegem, R (1999), Le rôle de la conscience du juge dans l'histoire du droit anglais, in J-M Carbasse & L Depambour-Tarride (sdd) (1999), *La conscience du juge dans la tradition juridique européenne* (Presses Universitaires de France, 1999) 263

Verkuil, PR (1975), The Ombudsman and the Limits of the Adversary System (1975) 75 *Columbia Law Review* 845

Vescovi, E (1980), Ordinary Proceedings in First Instance: Iberian Peninsula and Latin America, *International Encyclopedia of Comparative Law*, Volume XVI, Chapter 6, Part VI (JCB Mohr) (completed 1980)

Waddams, S (2003), *Dimensions of Private Law: Categories and Concepts in Anglo-American Legal Reasoning* (Cambridge University Press, 2003)

Waddams, S (2011), *Principle and Policy in Contract Law: Competing or Complementary Concepts?* (Cambridge University Press, 2011)

Watkin, TG (1997), *The Italian Legal Tradition* (Ashgate, 1997)

Weir, T (1971), The Common Law System, *International Encyclopedia of Comparative Law*, Volume II, Chapter 2, Part III (JCB Mohr) (completed 1971)

Weir, T (1992), Contracts in Rome and England (1992) 66 *Tulane Law Review* 1615

Weir, T (1998), The Staggering March of Negligence, in Cane & Stapleton (1998) 97

Weir, T (2006), *An Introduction to Tort Law* (Oxford University Press, 2nd edn, 2006)

Wijffels, A (2010), *Introduction historique au droit: France, Allemagne, Angleterre* (Presses Universitaires de France, 2010)

Woolf, H (Lord) (1996), *Access to Justice: Final Report to the Lord Chancellor on the Civil Justice System in England and Wales* (HMSO, July 1996)

Zakrzewski, R (2005), *Remedies Reclassified* (Oxford University Press, 2005)

Zander, M (2004), *The Law-Making Process* (Cambridge University Press, 6th edn, 2004)

Zander, M (2007), *Cases and Materials on the English Legal System* (Cambridge University Press, 10th edn, 2007)

Zweigert, K & Kötz, H (1998), *An Introduction to Comparative Law* (Oxford University Press, 3rd edn, 1998; trans T Weir)

Index